OLD FAVORITE
HONEY RECIPES

How to Substitute Honey for Sugar
in a Recipe

A general rule for substituting honey as a sweetener in a recipe that calls for sugar is this: Use honey in one-half the amount of sugar called for; that is, if a cup of sugar is listed, a half-cup of honey will provide the same degree of sweetening. When cooking with honey, remember that honey is a liquid. You may have to add more flour or reduce the amount of other liquid in a recipe to get the proper consistency in the final product. And when you substitute honey for sugar in a cake, bread or cookie recipe, lower the oven temperature by about 25° F so that the baked product will cook evenly inside and out.

American Honey Institute's

OLD FAVORITE
HONEY RECIPES

and the

HONEY RECIPES BOOK
of the
Iowa Honey Producers Association

Meyerbooks, Publisher
Glenwood, Illinois

ISBN 0-916638-17-0

Library of Congress Card No. 88-090602

Published by
Meyerbooks
P.O. Box 427
Glenwood, Illinois 60425

TABLE OF CONTENTS

OLD FAVORITE
HONEY RECIPES

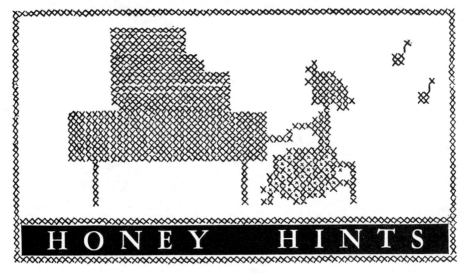

"Your food will have a sweeter taste
If you the viands do not waste;
And with each pay check if you try,
An extra U. S. bond to buy."

• Honey is a natural, unrefined food. It is unique in that it is the only unmanufactured sweet available in commercial quantities.

Since seventy-five to eighty per cent of its composition is sugars, honey has an energy-producing value second to few foods. Cane and beet sugars must be broken down into simpler sugars by digestive juices before they can be absorbed into the blood stream and assimilated into the tissues. These resulting simple sugars, dextrose and levulose, make up almost the entire sugar content of honey. It has been clinically demonstrated that little digestion is necessary and that absorption takes place quickly.

Honey Puts No Tax Upon Digestive System

• The word "sugar" to most people means the sugar of commerce, derived from sugar cane or sugar beets. To the chemist it is the name for a large variety of materials with varying degrees of chemical complexity and great variation in both uses and characteristics. As stated in the preceding paragraph, when ordinary cane sugar is digested, it is split into two simpler sugars, dextrose and levulose. A sugar of this category which splits into two simpler sugars is called a disaccharide. The simple sugars into which it is split are the monosaccharides.

The sugars of honey are primarily monosaccharides, that is, they require no digestive change before they can be absorbed. In honey also may be found small proportions of sucrose (cane sugar), traces of maltose (malt sugar) and sometimes also less well-known sugars. For example, melezitose (a trisaccharide sugar) has been found in some honey-dews derived usually from coniferous plants, and sugar alcohols have been found in other honey-dews. Naturally, our concern is chiefly with the sugars of honey which occur in amounts large enough to be significant.

Levulose has been called the queen of sugars. It is almost twice as sweet as cane sugar, and besides its sweetness, it carries to the human senses something that might almost be called a flavor. In a pure state this sugar is difficult to obtain, but it occurs naturally in mixtures with other sugars not only in honey but in many fruits. It dissolves in water readily and when dissolved, it crystallizes out only under circumstances that are difficult to produce, so that if one finds crystals in honey they are not crystals of levulose but of dextrose.

2

Dextrose (sometimes also called "*d*-glucose" but not to be confused with commercial glucose syrup) is a sugar of quite different nature. It is almost half as sweet as cane sugar, dissolves in about its own weight of water at ordinary temperatures, and crystallizes from a water solution quickly when it occurs in more than an amount equal to the water of solution. It is this sugar in honey that forms crystals. It should be noted that in an average honey the per cent of dextrose is roughly twice the per cent of water, hence we may expect that on standing, dextrose crystals will be thrown down. It is because of this that honeys granulate.

If crystals form in honey quickly, they are usually small, whereas if they form slowly, they are coarse. These differences involve no chemical differences, only a difference in the size of the crystals. On the market we find specially processed finely crystalline honey of smooth texture.

In addition to its sugars honey contains as its minor components a considerable number of mineral constituents, seven members of the B vitamin complex, ascorbic acid (vitamin C), dextrins, plant pigments, amino acids and other organic acids, traces of protein, esters and other aromatic compounds, and several enzymes.

The Average Chemical Composition of Honey

The Principal Components	Per Cent
Water	17.7
Levulose (fruit sugar)	40.5
Dextrose (grape sugar)	34.0
Sucrose (cane sugar)	1.9
Dextrins and gums	1.5
Ash (Silica, Iron, Copper, Manganese, Chlorine, Calcium, Potassium, Sodium, Phosphorus, Sulfur, Aluminum, Magnesium)	0.18
Total	95.78

Known Substances Difficult to Demonstrate Quantitatively:

Enzymes:
   Invertase (converts sucrose to dextrose and levulose), Diastase (converts starch to maltose), Catalase (decomposes hydrogen peroxide), Inulase (converts inulin to levulose)
Aromatic bodies (terpenes, aldehydes, esters)
Higher alcohols (mannitol, dulcitol, etc.)
Maltose, rare sugars (sometimes melezitose, etc.)
   In every 100 grams of honey there are 0.18 of a gram of mineral constituents.

Honey Contains Vitamins

• The vitamin content of honey about which there has been much discussion has recently been under laboratory study. Many of the earlier workers reported the absence of vitamins. This is not surprising since many foods relatively low in vitamins were given a similar rating because the then available methods did not detect small quantities of the vitamins. With the present improved procedures the vitamin content of any food material can be estimated with considerable accuracy. Extensive studies on the B vitamin content of honey have recently been made by Kitzes, Schuette, and Elvehjem.

While it is true that honey cannot be regarded as a real source of vitamins, on the other hand, it is not devoid of these dietary essentials. This means that when honey is consumed, it supplies, in small part, the vitamins needed for the metabolism of the sugar ingested from the honey. Since many of the B vitamins are used in the metabolism of sugar, we can calculate what part of the total requirement honey supplies for its metabolism by the body. It is found that honey supplies approximately 1/25 of the thiamine needed for utilization of its carbohydrate. Likewise the amount of riboflavin found in honey provides about ⅛ and the niacin 1/10 of the quantity required for metabolism of the sugar. Similar calculations cannot be made for pantothenic acid, pyridoxine, and biotin because the requirements for human beings are not known but small amounts of each of these vitamins are present in honey.

The following table shows the minimum daily requirement of thiamine, riboflavin, niacin, and ascorbic acid for an infant and the amount present in 100 grams of honey:

	Minimum daily requirement for infant	Amount present in 100 grams honey	Per cent of requirement
Thiamine	0.25 mg.	0.004 mg.	2
Riboflavin	0.50 mg.	0.028 mg.	5
Niacin	4.0 mg.	0.12 mg.	3
Ascorbic Acid	10.0 mg.	4.0 mg.	40

Honey Contains Minerals

• Among the mineral elements found in honey are iron, copper, sodium, potassium, manganese, calcium, magnesium and phosphorus. These minerals are all essential to good nutrition of animals. They are all present in honey, although in some cases only in trace quantities.

Honey is Suitable for Infant Feeding

• Honey is recognized as a satisfactory supplement to milk in infant feeding. Ask your physician to recommend a formula in which honey is included.

"Honey appears to have a special advantage in infant feeding. Since it is easily obtained, is very palatable, and digestible, honey would seem to be a form of carbohydrate which should have wider use in infant feeding.

"Bobs Roberts Memorial Hospital for Children is continually using honey in the clinic and finds it very successful."

Recent research has shown that "honey would seem to have a definite beneficial influence upon the retention of calcium by young infants."[1]

Honey is a Good Food for Growing Children

• Honey is a pleasant source of readily available energy for growing children. Since bacteria which cause diseases in human beings cannot live in honey, it is considered a safe and wholesome food.

Types of Honey

• There are a number of types of honey on the market today—liquid, comb, chunk and cut comb, and solid (sometimes called granulated or finely crystallized).

Weight of Honey

• A cup of honey weighs 12 ounces of which not quite 1/5 is moisture. This yields approximately 9¼ ounces of carbohydrate as compared with the 7 ounces contained in a cup of sugar. Honey contains more carbohydrate than the same measure of cane sugar.

----

[1] Knott, E. M., Shukers, C. F., Schultz, F. W., The Effect of Honey upon Calcium Retentions in Infants. Journal of Pediatrics 19; 485–494, 1941.

To measure honey

• Measure shortening first, and then measure honey in the same measuring unit.

To store honey

• Keep liquid honey in a dry place. Freezing does not injure the color or flavor but may hasten granulation. Avoid damp places for storage because honey has the property of absorbing and retaining moisture. Do not put honey in the refrigerator.

To liquefy honey that has granulated or solidified

• Place the container in a bowl of warm water—not warmer than the hand can bear—until all crystals are melted. See that the honey container does not rest on the bottom of the water container.

To purchase honey

• Select the flavor you desire. The flavor depends upon the kind of flowers from which the bees gather nectar. Honey producers frequently mix several honeys by heating moderately and stirring to produce a blend with a flavor which is most satisfactory. If you have storage space, it is more economical to buy honey in large size containers.

To serve honey

• You may secure a honey container with a top that cuts the flow of honey and leaves no drip or stickiness. Individual containers are liked by children.

To replace sugar with honey in a cake or cooky recipe that calls for all sugar

• A general rule is to reduce the amount of liquid $\frac{1}{4}$ cup for each cup of honey used to replace sugar.

Cakes and cookies made with honey are noted for their keeping qualities. The ability of honey to absorb and retain moisture and thus retard the drying out and staling of baked goods is of great importance to the homemaker who wishes to do her baking in advance. This property combined with the food value and flavor of honey is valuable also to the baker.

Measurements and Ingredients in General

1. Read the recipe carefully.
2. Assemble all ingredients and utensils before starting to mix.
3. Grease pans that are to be greased.
4. Measure ingredients accurately with standard measuring cups and measuring spoons.
5. Follow directions in recipe.
6. Sift flour once before measuring. Pile lightly in standard measuring cup (do not shake down), level off with straight edge of knife.
7. Flour containing husks or bran coats like cornmeal, graham, or bran are mixed in, not sifted.
8. Use amount of baking powder that directions on baking powder container specify.
9. The amount of soda needed to neutralize the acidity in one cup of the average honey is 1/12 to 1/5 teaspoon. When sour milk and honey appear in a recipe, it is not necessary to add any extra soda for the honey.
10. Unless specified, the honey is in liquid form. Granulated honey may be used with equal success in any combination that is heated.

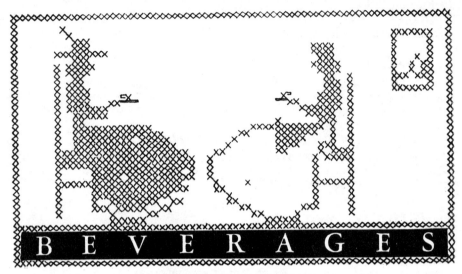

B E V E R A G E S

"A drink that tastes of honey sweet
Will always make a gracious treat."

Coffee

(medium strong)
2 level tablespoons coffee
1 cup boiling water

(strong)
3 level tablespoons coffee
1 cup boiling water

• Put the coffee into the pot with a little egg white or a crushed egg shell. Add a little cold water and stir all together thoroughly. Measure boiling water and add to the coffee. Place over the heat for three minutes. Turn off heat and let settle. Serve with honey.

Tea

• Scald a china or earthen teapot. Allow one teaspoon of tea to each cup of freshly-boiled water. Pour boiling water over tea. Allow to steep 3 minutes. Serve at once with honey.

Honey Cocoa Sirup

1¼ cup cocoa

1   cup sugar

½ teaspoon salt

⅛ teaspoon ground allspice

⅛ teaspoon ground cinnamon

1½ cups boiling water

½ cup honey

2   teaspoons vanilla extract

• Combine cocoa, sugar, salt, and spices. Add boiling water. Blend. Place over low heat, bring to a boil and boil 5 minutes, stirring constantly. Remove from fire. Cool. Add honey and vanilla. Store in covered jar in refrigerator until ready to use. Approximate yield: 2¼ cups.
To serve: Heat ¼ cup Honey Cocoa Sirup with 2 cups scalded milk over boiling water. Before serving, beat with rotary beater. Yield: 3 servings. Honey gives this sirup an unusual smoothness and a delicious flavor in addition to extra food value.

Lemonade

• Mix 2 tablespoons of honey with the juice of ½ lemon. Stir well. Add 1 cup hot or cold water according to whether hot or cold drink is desired.

Russian Tea (45 cups)

1 box stick cinnamon (1¼ ounces)

1 box whole cloves (1¼ ounces)

¾ cup honey

3 oranges, juice of 3 and grated rind of 1

6 lemons, juice of 6 and grated rind of 1

⅓ cup black tea

5 quarts water, boiling

• Cook spices, honey and grated rind with 2 cups water for 10 minutes. Let stand 1 hour. Strain. Steep tea in the boiling water 1 minute. Then add fruit juice and spice mixture. Serve hot.

Refreshing Party Drink

1 quart currants

1 pint water

1 cup honey

1 small stick cinnamon

5 oranges

3 lemons

water

• Wash currants, place in a kettle and cover with water. Reserve ¼ cup currants for garnishing. Simmer gently for 10 minutes. Strain. If a clear juice is desired, do not press the pulp. Combine the pint of water, honey, and cinnamon and boil for 5 minutes. Remove the spice stick. Combine the juice of the oranges, lemons, and currant juice with the spiced sirup, diluted to taste. Fresh pineapple or cranberry juice may be used instead of orange and lemon juice. Serve hot or cold.

Grape Juice

• Mix 2 tablespoons honey with ¼ cup of boiling water. Stir until dissolved. Add enough hot grape juice to fill glass. 2 tablespoons of lemon juice may be added for variety. This makes a delicious cold weather drink.

Milk

• For extra flavor and nourishment add 2 tablespoons of honey to a glass of milk. Serve hot or cold.

Honey Eggnog

4 to 6 egg yolks

4 tablespoons honey

4 cups milk

nutmeg

• Beat the yolks of eggs until lemon colored. Add honey and mix well. Add milk slowly. Fill glasses. Add a slight grating of nutmeg. Serve at once.

To make an Orange Eggnog, replace milk with orange juice. Omit nutmeg.

7

BREADS

*"If I had all of Croesus' money
I'd still subsist on bread and honey."*

Enriched Bread (2 loaves)

2 cups milk or 1 cup milk and
    1 cup water

1 tablespoon salt

2 tablespoons shortening

2 tablespoons honey

1 cake compressed or dry
    granular yeast

6 cups enriched flour (about)

• Scald milk and cool to lukewarm. Add salt and shortening. Put honey and yeast in mixing bowl; let stand until yeast is softened. Add milk and half the flour. Beat thoroughly. Gradually add enough flour to make a soft dough. Turn out on floured board and knead until smooth and elastic. This requires about 8 minutes. Place in slightly-greased bowl and let rise until double in bulk. Punch down lightly and let rise again. Form into loaves. Place in greased pans. Allow to rise until double in bulk. If baked in individual loaves (one pound), bake 40 minutes at 400–425° F.

Whole Wheat Bread (2 loaves)

2 cups milk or 1 cup milk
    and 1 cup water

1 tablespoon salt

¼ cup shortening

¼ cup honey

1 cake compressed or dry
    granular yeast

5½ cups (about) whole wheat
    flour, finely ground

• Scald milk and cool to lukewarm. Add salt and shortening. Put honey and yeast in mixing bowl; let stand until yeast is softened. Add milk and 2 cups whole wheat flour. Beat thoroughly. Add another cup of flour and beat again. Add remainder of flour. Turn out on floured board and knead until no longer sticky. This requires about 8 minutes. Place in slightly-greased bowl and let rise until double in bulk. Punch down lightly and let rise again. Shape into two loaves and place in greased pans. Let rise until double in bulk. Bake at 375° F. for about 50 minutes or until nicely browned and loaf begins to shrink from the pan. Keep dough at even temperature (85° F.) for rising.

Honey Oatmeal Bread (3 loaves)

1½ cups milk
1 cup quick cooking oatmeal
2 tablespoons shortening
1 can evaporated milk
   (13 oz. size)
¼ cup honey
1 tablespoon salt
1 or 2 cakes compressed or
   dry granular yeast
2 cups flour
3 cups whole wheat flour
   (about)

• Boil milk, add oatmeal, and cook 2 minutes. Add shortening. When melted, add evaporated milk, honey and salt. Cool to lukewarm (98° F.), add crumbled yeast and let stand 2 minutes. Add flour and beat well. Add whole wheat flour to form a soft dough. Knead until mixture is smooth (about 8 minutes). Let rise until double in bulk, form into 3 loaves. Let loaves rise until double in bulk, and bake at 375° F. for 45–50 minutes.

Orange Nut Bread

2 tablespoons shortening
1 cup honey
1 egg
1½ tablespoons grated orange
   rind
¾ cup orange juice
2¼ cups flour
2½ teaspoons baking powder
⅛ teaspoon soda
½ teaspoon salt
¾ cup chopped nut meats

• Cream the shortening and honey well. Add the beaten egg and orange rind. Sift the dry ingredients and add alternately with the orange juice. Add chopped nuts. Pour into greased loaf pan, the bottom of which has been lined with waxed paper. Bake at 325° F. for 1 hour or until the loaf is nicely browned and begins to shrink from the pan. Yield: 1 loaf.

Nut Bread

½ cup shortening
½ cup sugar
½ cup honey
1 egg
3 cups sifted flour
3 teaspoons baking powder
1 teaspoon salt
¾ cup milk
1 cup chopped nuts

• Cream together shortening and sugar. Add honey and mix thoroughly. Add egg, beating well. Sift together flour, baking powder, and salt. Add to creamed mixture alternately with milk. Add nuts. Bake in greased loaf pan in moderate oven (350° F.) 1¼ hours. Yield: 1 loaf.

Corn Bread

¾ cup cornmeal
1 cup flour
3 teaspoons baking powder
½ teaspoon salt
1 cup milk
¼ cup honey
1 egg
2 tablespoons melted butter

• Mix dry ingredients. Add milk, honey, and beaten egg. Add melted butter last. Bake 25 minutes in a buttered shallow pan in hot oven (400°F.). Serve with honey.

Honey Currant Cake

1 cake compressed or dry granular yeast

¼ cup lukewarm water

½ cup milk

¼ cup honey

1 teaspoon salt

¼ cup melted shortening

1 egg

2 cups sifted enriched flour (about)

½ cup currants

• Soften yeast in lukewarm water. Scald milk and cool to lukewarm. Add honey, salt, shortening. Beat egg and add. Blend thoroughly. Add 1 cup flour and beat well. Add softened yeast. Add currants and remaining flour to make a moderately stiff drop batter. Beat until smooth. Cover and let rise until bubbly (about 1 hour). Stir down, pour into greased pan 8 x 8 x 2-inches, filling pan about half full. Spread batter with honey (4 tablespoons). Sprinkle ¼ teaspoon cinnamon and ¼ cup chopped nuts over honey. Let rise until double in bulk. Bake in moderate oven (375° F.) 35 to 40 minutes. (May also be baked as muffins, 20 to 25 minutes). Yield: 1 cake, 8 x 8-inches, or 1½ dozen 2-inch muffins.

Refrigerator Rolls

½ cup honey

1 cake compressed or dry granular yeast

½ cup mashed potatoes

2 cups milk and potato water

1 tablespoon salt

5 cups flour (about)

½ cup melted shortening

• Combine honey and yeast and let stand to soften yeast. Add mashed potatoes to scalded milk and water. Cool to lukewarm. Combine yeast and liquid mixture. Add salt, half the flour, and beat thoroughly. Add melted shortening and remainder of flour to make a soft dough. Knead. Let rise until double in bulk. Punch down, and put in a cold place for 24 hours or more, or shape at once, and put in a warm place to rise. Bake at 425° F. for 15 to 20 minutes. Note: If dough in refrigerator rises, punch down. This dough will keep 4 or 5 days.
Put 3 small balls of dough in greased muffin pans for clover leaf rolls.

Pecan Rolls

½ cup butter or margarine

1 cup honey

1 cup pecan halves

sweet roll dough

• When sweet dough is light, punch down and let rest a few minutes. Roll out in sheet one-half inch thick. Brush with butter and spread with honey. Roll as a jelly roll and seal edge firmly. Cut into one-inch slices. In bottom of the baking pan place butter cut into small pieces. Spread honey over this and scatter on the pecans. Place rolls one inch apart on the honey and butter mixture. Cover and let rise until double in bulk. Bake in moderate oven (375° F.) 20 to 25 minutes. Let rolls stand in pans one minute after baking before turning them out. If greased muffin pans are used, place ½ teaspoon butter and 1 teaspoon honey in each muffin cup.

Sweet Rolls

1 cup milk

¼ cup honey

¼ cup shortening

1 teaspoon salt

2 cakes compressed or dry granular yeast

¼ cup lukewarm water

2 eggs

5 cups flour (about)

● Scald milk. Add honey, shortening, and salt. Soften yeast in lukewarm water and add to milk mixture. Add beaten eggs and half the flour. Beat well. Add rest of flour. Mix well. Knead on a slightly-floured board until smooth. Place in slightly-greased bowl. Cover and let rise until double in bulk. Punch down and form into rolls or coffee cake. Let rise again. Bake at 400–425° F. 20–25 minutes.

Honey Rolls

1 cup milk

¼ cup shortening

½ cup honey

1 cake compressed or dry granular yeast softened in ¼ cup lukewarm water

1½ teaspoons salt

4 cups flour

1 egg

● Scald milk, add shortening and honey, cool to lukewarm. Add yeast, salt and 2 cups of flour. Add beaten egg and remainder of flour to form a soft dough. Knead lightly until smooth. Let rise twice, then form into rolls. Let rolls rise until light. Bake at 400° F. about 20 minutes.

Quick Coffee Cake

1½ cups sifted flour

2 teaspoons baking powder

½ teaspoon salt

1 egg

⅔ cup milk

⅓ cup honey

3 tablespoons melted shortening

● Sift together dry ingredients. Beat egg. Add milk, honey, and melted shortening. Stir into dry ingredients. Mix lightly (only enough to moisten flour). Spread in lightly greased 8-inch square pan. Cover batter with Honey Topping. Bake in hot oven (400° F.) 25 to 30 minutes.

Honey Topping

¼ cup butter or margarine

¼ cup sugar

¼ cup sifted flour

¼ cup honey

¼ cup chopped nuts

● Cream butter or margarine. Add sugar, flour, and honey and mix thoroughly. Sprinkle with nut meats.

11

Waffles

2 cups flour

3 teaspoons baking powder

½ teaspoon salt

1½ cups milk

2 tablespoons honey

2 eggs

½ cup melted shortening

• Sift dry ingredients. Combine milk, honey, egg yolks, shortening, and add to dry ingredients. Fold in stiffly beaten egg whites. Bake in hot waffle iron.

Serve with the following: Heat 1 cup honey in top of double boiler. Add ⅛ to ¼ cup butter and ¼ teaspoon cinnamon, if desired. Serve warm.

Honey French Toast

2 eggs

1 pint milk

¼ cup honey

½ teaspoon salt

    a sprinkling of mace or nutmeg

6 or 8 slices of bread several days old

• Beat eggs until light. Warm the milk slightly and blend well with the honey. Add the salt, mace, and beaten eggs and stir well. Cut bread about one-half inch thick. Dip each slice into the milk and egg mixture and place on a hot well-greased griddle. Brown well on both sides. Serve with honey.

Honey Milk Toast

2 cups hot milk

½ teaspoon salt

1 tablespoon butter

6 slices buttered toast

• Spread each slice of buttered hot toast with honey. Heat milk just to the boiling point, add salt and butter. Keep hot until ready to serve and then pour over the honey spread toast. Serve at once before toast loses its crispness.

Honey Cinnamon Toast

• Toast slices of bread on one side. While still hot, butter the untoasted side of bread. Spread buttered side with honey. Sprinkle cinnamon over the top. Place slices under broiler flame until the bread is well browned and the dressing is well blended.

Honey Orange Muffins

½ cup sifted flour

½ teaspoon salt

2 teaspoons baking powder

½ cup whole wheat flour

1 egg, well beaten

¼ cup orange juice

1 teaspoon grated orange rind

½ cup honey

3 tablespoons melted shortening

• Sift flour, salt, and baking powder together. Add whole wheat flour and mix thoroughly. Combine egg, orange juice and rind, honey, and shortening. Add all at once to flour, stirring only enough to dampen all flour. Bake in well-greased muffin pans in moderately hot oven (400° F.) 15 to 20 minutes, or until browned.

Corn Muffins

¾ cup sifted flour
1¼ teaspoons baking powder
½ teaspoon salt
⅛ cup cornmeal
¼ cup prepared apple
1 egg, well beaten
⅛ cup milk
¼ cup honey
3 tablespoons shortening, melted

• Sift flour once, measure, add baking powder and salt, and sift again. Add cornmeal. Wash, pare, and cut apples into eighths. Remove core and cut crosswise into very thin slices. Combine egg, milk, honey, and shortening. Add all at once to flour-cornmeal mixture, stirring only enough to dampen all flour. Fold in apple. Bake in well-greased 2-inch muffin pans in hot oven (400° F.) for 20 minutes, or until done. Approximate yield: 8–12 muffins.

Bran Raisin Muffins

1 cup flour
4 teaspoons baking powder
½ teaspoon salt
¾ cup bran
½ cup seeded raisins
½ cup milk
4 tablespoons honey
2 tablespoons shortening, melted
1 egg, beaten

• Sift flour, baking powder, and salt together; stir in bran and add raisins. Combine the milk, honey, melted shortening, and beaten egg. Add dry ingredients. Stir just enough to moisten the flour. Pour into greased muffin pans and bake in moderately hot oven at 425° F. for 25 minutes.

Honey Muffins with Variations

2 cups flour
1 teaspoon salt
3 teaspoons baking powder
1 cup milk
4 tablespoons honey
1 egg, beaten
¼ cup melted shortening

• Sift flour with salt and baking powder. Mix milk, honey, beaten egg, and melted shortening. Add to dry mixture. Stir quickly just long enough to moisten dry ingredients. Fill greased muffin pans one-half full. Bake in a moderately hot oven (400° F.) 25 to 30 minutes or until delicately browned.

Variations

BLUEBERRY MUFFINS _____ Add ½ cup fresh blueberries to sifted dry ingredients.

FRUIT MUFFINS _____ Add ½ cup chopped citron, ¼ cup chopped maraschino cherries to batter. Brush muffins lightly with honey before baking.

HONEY MUFFINS _____ Put 1 teaspoon finely crystallized honey in center of batter of each muffin.

PEANUT BUTTER MUFFINS ____ Blend ¼ cup peanut butter with honey before adding to milk and egg mixture.

SOYBEAN MUFFINS _____ Replace ½ cup flour with ½ cup soybean flour.

WHOLE WHEAT MUFFINS _____ Replace 1 cup of flour with 1 cup of whole wheat flour.

C A K E S

"With butter, egg and good honey
Your cake will moist and flaky be."

Honey Angel Food

1   teaspoon cream of tartar
½   teaspoon salt
1   cup egg whites (8 to 10 whites)
¾   cup sugar
1   cup cake flour
½   cup honey
½   teaspoon grated lemon rind

• Add the cream of tartar and salt to the egg whites in a bowl. Beat the whites with a wire whip until they are stiff. They should move only slightly when the bowl is tipped. Fold one half the sugar slowly into the egg whites 2 tablespoons at a time. Sift the remaining sugar with the flour and add later. The ½ cup honey must be warmed so that it will be thin and will pour in a fine stream over the egg whites as the egg whites are folded in. After the honey is added, fold in the flour and sugar mixture, sifting ¼ cup over the whites at a time. Add grated lemon rind. Pour the mixture into an angel food pan and bake at a temperature of 300° F. for 50 minutes. Invert the pan, cool and remove to a cake rack.

Chocolate Honey Angel Food Cake

¾   cup sifted cake flour
¼   cup cocoa
1   cup sifted granulated sugar
1   cup egg whites (8 to 10 whites)
¼   teaspoon salt
¾   teaspoon cream of tartar
1   teaspoon vanilla extract
⅛   cup honey

• Sift flour once, measure, add cocoa and ¼ cup of the sugar, and sift together 4 times. Beat egg whites and salt with rotary beater or flat wire whisk. When foamy, add cream of tartar and vanilla. Continue beating until eggs are stiff enough to hold up in peaks, but not dry. Add remaining ¾ cup of sugar, 2 tablespoons at a time, beating after each addition until sugar is just blended. Add honey, 2 tablespoons at a time, beating after each addition until honey is just blended. Sift about ¼ cup flour-sugar mixture over egg whites and fold in lightly; repeat until all flour is used. Turn into ungreased angel food pan. Cut gently through batter with knife to remove air bubbles. Bake in slow oven (325° F.) 1 hour. Remove from oven and invert pan 1 hour, or until cold.

14

Super Delicious Chocolate Cake

3   squares unsweetened chocolate, melted

⅔ cup honey

1¾ cups sifted cake flour

1   teaspoon soda

¾ teaspoon salt

½ cup butter or other shortening

½ cup sugar

1   teaspoon vanilla extract

2   eggs, unbeaten

⅔ cup water

• Blend chocolate and honey; cool to lukewarm. Sift flour once, measure, add soda and salt, and sift together three times. Cream butter thoroughly, add sugar gradually, and cream together until light and fluffy. Add chocolate-honey mixture and vanilla. Blend. Add eggs, one at a time, beating thoroughly after each addition. Add flour, alternately with water, a small amount at a time, beating after each addition until smooth. Bake in two greased 8-inch layer pans in moderate oven (350° F.) 30 to 35 minutes. Spread with French Honey-Chocolate Frosting.

French Honey-Chocolate Frosting

½ cup sugar

¼ cup butter

¼ cup light cream

¼ cup honey

¼ teaspoon salt

3   squares unsweetened chocolate, cut into small pieces

2   egg yolks, well beaten

• Combine sugar, butter, cream, honey, salt, and chocolate in top of double boiler. Place over boiling water. When chocolate is melted, beat with rotary beater until blended. Pour small amount of mixture over egg yolks, stirring vigorously. Return to double boiler and cook 2 minutes longer, or until mixture thickens slightly, stirring constantly. Remove from hot water, place in pan of ice water or cracked ice, and beat until of right consistency to spread. Yield: Frosting to cover tops and sides of 2 (8-inch) layers.

Orange Honey Cake

2   cups sifted cake flour

3½ teaspoons baking powder

¾ teaspoon salt

½ cup butter or other shortening

½ cup sugar

⅔ cup honey

2   egg yolks

½ cup orange juice

2   egg whites, stiffly beaten

• Sift flour once, measure, add baking powder and salt, and sift together three times. Cream butter thoroughly, add sugar gradually, and cream together until light and fluffy. Add honey. Blend. Add egg yolks and beat thoroughly. Add flour, alternately with orange juice, a small amount at a time, beating after each addition until smooth. Fold in egg whites. Bake in two greased 9-inch layer pans in moderate oven (350° F.) 30 to 35 minutes.

Boiled Honey Frosting

1½ cups honey

⅛ teaspoon salt

2   egg whites

• Cook honey and salt to 238° F. or until it will spin a thread, or make a soft ball when dropped into cold water. Beat egg whites. Pour the hot honey in a thin stream over the beaten egg whites continuing to beat until all honey is added and frosting will stand in peaks. Spread on cake.

Honey Ginger Cake

2½ cups sifted cake flour
1 teaspoon soda
½ teaspoon baking powder
1 teaspoon salt
1 teaspoon ground ginger
1 teaspoon ground cinnamon
½ cup butter
½ cup brown sugar, firmly packed
1 egg, unbeaten
1 cup honey
1 cup sour milk or buttermilk

• Sift flour once, measure, add soda, baking powder, salt, and spices, and sift together three times. Cream butter thoroughly, add sugar gradually, and cream together until light and fluffy. Add egg and beat thoroughly. Add honey and blend. Add flour, alternately with sour milk, a small amount at a time, beating after each addition until smooth. Bake in two well-greased 9-inch layer pans in moderate oven (350° F.) 45 minutes or until done.
Note: If baked in paper-lined cup cake pans, bake at 350° F. for 30 minutes.

Uncooked Honey Frosting

⅛ teaspoon salt
1 egg white
½ cup honey
½ teaspoon flavoring

• Add salt to egg white. Warm honey over hot water. Pour in a thin stream over egg white while beating vigorously. Add flavoring. Continue to beat until thick and fluffy.

Frosting with Chopped Apricots

• To boiled Honey Frosting add ⅔ cup of well washed, chopped dried apricots. Add ¼ teaspoon each of almond and lemon extract. This frosting gives a new flavor to a light cake.

Honey Fruit Cake

2 cups butter or other shortening
1½ cups brown sugar
1 cup honey
9 eggs
4 cups flour
1 teaspoon soda
1 teaspoon cinnamon
1 teaspoon mace
3 tablespoons milk
2 pounds seeded raisins
2 pounds currants
1 pound nut meats (almonds if available)
1 pound candied citron
1 pound candied orange
1 pound candied lemon
candied cherries and candied rhubarb if desired

• Cream butter, add sugar and honey and cream well. Add well beaten eggs, flour, soda and spices that have been sifted together. Add milk. Add the slightly floured fruit that has been carefully washed and dried in oven, almonds that have been blanched and dried, candied fruit cut in pieces. Mix well and place in pans that have been lined with greased brown paper. Decorate top of cake with cherries, almonds and strips of citron. Place greased paper over top of cake. Steam for 2½ hours and then bake in a slow oven (250°F.) for 2½ hours.

Honey Layer Cake

½ cup shortening

½ cup sugar

½ cup honey

2 egg yolks

2 cups sifted cake flour

3 teaspoons baking powder

¾ teaspoon salt

¾ cup milk

½ teaspoon flavoring

2 egg whites

• Cream shortening thoroughly. Add sugar and honey, beat until mixture is light and fluffy. Add egg yolks and beat well. Add sifted dry ingredients alternately with milk. Add flavoring and fold in stiffly-beaten egg whites. Bake in 2 layers at 350° F. for 30 minutes.

Note: Spread Lemon, Fig, or Orange Filling between layers. If you desire a Chocolate Flake Cake, fold in with the beaten egg whites 1 cup chocolate flakes made by cutting unsweetened chocolate finely, or putting chocolate through meat grinder.

Lemon Filling

¼ cup sugar

2 tablespoons flour

¼ cup lemon juice

½ cup honey

  grated rind of 1 lemon

1 egg, slightly beaten

1 tablespoon butter

• Mix ingredients in top of double boiler. Cook over hot water, stirring constantly until thickened. Cool. Spread between layers of cake.

Fig Filling

½ cup chopped figs

½ cup honey

¼ cup water

2 tablespoons orange juice

1 tablespoon corn starch

• Mix ingredients in top of double boiler and cook until thick enough to spread. Spread between cake layers while hot.

Orange Filling

2 tablespoons sugar

2 tablespoons flour

½ tablespoon lemon juice

½ cup orange juice

¼ cup honey

  grated rind of 1 orange

1 egg, slightly beaten

1 tablespoon butter

• Mix ingredients in top of double boiler and cook until thickened. Cool and spread between cake layers.

17

Loaf Cake

⅔ cup shortening

1½ cups honey

3 eggs

3 cups flour

3 teaspoons baking powder

½ teaspoon salt

1 teaspoon cinnamon

1 teaspoon mace

½ cup fruit juice

1 cup seeded raisins

1 cup chopped nuts

• Cream shortening, add honey gradually. Blend well. Add well-beaten eggs. Sift dry ingredients together. Add alternately with the fruit juice. Stir in raisins and nuts. Pour into 2 loaf pans lined with well-greased waxed paper. Bake 1 hour in moderate oven (350° F.).

Applesauce Cake

⅓ cup shortening

¾ cup honey

2 cups flour

¼ teaspoon cloves

½ teaspoon cinnamon

½ teaspoon nutmeg

¼ teaspoon salt

1 teaspoon soda

1 cup cold, unsweetened applesauce

1 cup seedless raisins

• Cream shortening. Add honey gradually, creaming after each addition. Mix and sift together dry ingredients and add alternately with the applesauce to the creamed mixture. Fold in raisins. Pour batter into a well-greased 8 x 8-inch pan. Bake in a moderate oven (350° F.) for about 45 minutes.

Everyday Cake

⅓ cup shortening

½ cup sugar

½ cup honey

1 egg

½ cup milk

2 cups sifted cake flour

2 teaspoons baking powder

¼ teaspoon salt

1 teaspoon lemon extract

• Cream shortening. Add sugar and cream well. Add honey and beat until light and fluffy. Add egg and beat thoroughly. Add sifted dry ingredients alternately with milk. Add extract. Bake in two layers in moderate oven (375° F.) 25 to 30 minutes. Put layers together with French Honey-Chocolate Frosting.

Honey Sour Cream Spice Cup Cakes

½ cup shortening

1 cup brown sugar

1 cup honey

3 egg yolks

2 cups flour

¼ teaspoon salt

1 teaspoon ground cloves

1 teaspoon allspice

1 teaspoon cinnamon

1 teaspoon soda

1 cup thick sour cream

3 egg whites

• Cream shortening. Add sugar and honey and cream well again. Add egg yolks, one at a time, and beat well. Sift dry ingredients and add alternately with the sour cream, beating after each addition. Fold in stiffly-beaten whites of eggs. Bake in greased muffin pans in a moderate oven (350° F.) 30 minutes, or in a greased cake pan for 40 minutes.

Note: If brown sugar becomes hard, put it in the bread box over night.

Nut Cake

½ cup shortening

1 cup sugar

½ cup honey

¾ cup cold water

2 cups sifted cake flour

1 cup broken nut meats

4 egg whites

4 teaspoons baking powder

1 teaspoon lemon extract

• Cream shortening and sugar. Add honey. Beat well. Add flour and cold water alternately. Add half the beaten egg whites. Add the nut meats floured slightly. Fold in remainder of beaten eggs, baking powder and extract. Bake in 9 x 12-inch cake pan (350° F.) 50 to 60 minutes. Frost with uncooked Honey Frosting.

Gold Cake

¼ cup butter or margarine

½ cup honey

1 teaspoon orange extract

1 cup sifted flour

1½ teaspoons baking powder

½ teaspoon salt

4 egg yolks

¼ cup milk

• Cream butter or margarine. Add honey gradually and beat well. Add extract. Sift together flour, baking powder, and salt. Add ¼ of the sifted dry ingredients. Add eggs and beat well. Add remaining ingredients. Bake 40–45 minutes in greased loaf pan in moderate oven (350° F.).

Honey Meringue

1 egg white

½ cup honey

• Beat egg white with rotary or electric beater until it begins to froth. Then add honey, gradually beating until meringue stands high in peaks, (from 5 to 10 minutes beating). Use on puddings or cakes.

Spice Cake

½ cup shortening
¾ cup honey
2 cups sifted cake flour
2 teaspoons baking powder
½ teaspoon salt
1 teaspoon cinnamon
½ teaspoon cloves
¼ teaspoon nutmeg
2 eggs, separated
½ cup milk
½ cup broken nut meats
½ cup chopped raisins

• Cream shortening, add honey and beat thoroughly. Mix and sift together flour, baking powder, salt, and spices. Add about 1 cup of sifted dry ingredients to shortening and honey mixture. Beat well. Add egg yolks and beat. Add remaining dry ingredients alternately with milk. Add nuts and raisins with last addition of flour. Stir in stiffly-beaten egg whites. Pour batter into greased tube pan. Bake in moderate oven (350° F.) 60 minutes, or until done.

Ginger Bread

2 cups sifted flour
2 teaspoons baking powder
1 teaspoon salt
½ teaspoon ginger
½ teaspoon cloves
½ teaspoon nutmeg
½ cup shortening
⅛ cup sugar
½ cup honey
2 eggs
¾ cup milk

• Combine first seven ingredients and sift together three times. Cream shortening. Add sugar and honey and beat well. Add ½ cup of sifted dry ingredients and mix thoroughly. Add beaten eggs. Add remainder of dry ingredients alternately with milk. Bake in greased pan (375° F.) about 35 to 40 minutes. Cut into squares, and top with honey meringue.

Tutti Frutti Cake

1 cup cooked prunes
1¾ cups seedless raisins
½ cup sliced citron
⅛ cup sliced candied
    lemon peel
½ cup sliced candied
    orange peel
½ cup sliced candied cherries
2 teaspoons cinnamon
1 teaspoon mace
½ teaspoon cloves
½ teaspoon allspice
1 cup prune juice
½ cup orange juice
1 cup honey
1 cup shortening
1 cup sugar
4 eggs
1 cup broken walnut meats
5 cups sifted flour
1½ teaspoons salt
1¼ teaspoons soda

• Remove pits from prunes and cut into small pieces. Rinse and drain raisins. Combine fruits and peels with spices, cover with fruit liquids and honey, blend well, and let stand over night. Cream shortening with sugar, add well-beaten eggs, and combine with fruit mixture and nuts. Add flour sifted with salt and soda, and blend thoroughly. Pour into greased paper-lined tube pan (about 10 x 4-inches). Bake in slow oven (300° F.) 3 to 3¼ hours. Before removing from oven, test with cake tester. Makes about 5 lbs. baked.

20

CANDIES

*"All candy calls for flavor sweet
And honey therein can't be beat."*

• If the essential rules are mastered, homemade candy can equal candy made by professionals, in flavor, consistency, and appearance.

The essential rules are:

1. Use a candy thermometer as the cold water test is not accurate enough.
2. Creamy candies should not be stirred until sugar is dissolved.
3. Use cooking utensils that are smooth on the inside.
4. Creamy candies, like fudge, should be cooled before beating.
5. Taffies and brittles should be stirred only enough to prevent burning.
6. Sugar crystals which form on the inside of the pan can be brushed down with a fork wrapped in cheesecloth and dipped in cold water.
7. As soon as caramels have cooled, wrap in waxed paper.
8. Penuchi and fudge should be stored in tightly covered containers.

• Candy sirup is cooked to one of five stages, depending upon the kind of candy being made:

Soft Ball	236° to 240° F.
Firm Ball	242° to 248° F.
Hard Ball	250° to 265° F.
Brittle	270° to 290° F.
Very Brittle	295° to 310° F.

Honey Fudge

2 cups sugar
1 square unsweetened chocolate
¼ teaspoon salt
1 cup evaporated milk
¼ cup honey
2 tablespoons butter
1 cup nuts

• Boil sugar, chocolate, salt, and milk for five minutes. Add honey and cook to soft-ball stage (240° F.). Add butter; let stand until lukewarm; beat until creamy, add nuts, and pour into buttered pan. Cut when firm.

Honey Fondant

⅔ cup honey
4 cups sugar
2 cups boiling water

● Cook honey, sugar, and water slowly. Do not let boil until sugar is dissolved. Keep crystals off side of the pan with cloth wet in cold water and wrapped around a fork. When sugar is dissolved, bring to a boil and boil slowly to the soft-ball stage (238° F.). Keeping a cover on the pan part of the time helps to keep the crystals from forming. Remove from fire and pour at once on large buttered platters. When lukewarm stir until creamy. Knead until smooth. Fondant improves if allowed to stand a few days before using. Flavor as desired.

Honey Caramels

2 cups sugar
2 cups honey
   few grains of salt
½ cup butter
1 cup evaporated milk

● Cook sugar, honey, and salt rapidly to hard-ball stage (250° F.). Stir occasionally. Add butter and milk gradually so the mixture does not stop boiling at any time. Cook rapidly to hard-ball stage (250° F.). Stir constantly so mixture will not stick. Pour into buttered pan and cool thoroughly before cutting into squares. Wrap individually in oiled paper.

Honey Divinity

2 cups sugar
⅛ cup honey
⅛ cup water
2 egg whites
½ cup chopped nut meats

● Boil sugar, honey, and water until sirup spins a thread (278° F.). Pour sirup over well-beaten egg whites, beating continuously. Just before mixture starts to set, add chopped nut meats. When mixture crystallizes, drop with a spoon on waxed paper.

Variation: Candied cherries or candied rhubarb may be added.

Honey Taffy

2 cups sugar
2 cups honey
⅔ cup cold water
⅛ teaspoon salt

● Boil sugar, honey, and water to brittle stage (288° F.). Add salt. Put in buttered dish to cool; pull until white.

Honey Bittersweets

Comb honey
hot water
confectioners' chocolate

● Let comb honey remain in refrigerator 24 hours before using. Cut comb honey into pieces about ¾ inch long and ⅜ inch wide with knife that is dipped in boiling water. Place pieces on trays covered with waxed paper; chill 30 minutes. Coat with dipping chocolate. Drop a nut on each piece. (It requires a little practice to be able to turn out honeyed bittersweets that do not develop honey leaks.) It is necessary to have dipping chocolate at proper temperature (about 70 to 75° F.) when coating. Coating in a room of 60 to 65° F. will cause the chocolate to harden more quickly.

Spiced Honey Nuts

3 cups sifted confectioners' sugar

3 teaspoons ground cinnamon

1½ teaspoons ground nutmeg

1½ teaspoons ground allspice

1 egg white, unbeaten

2 tablespoons honey

⅛ teaspoon salt

¾ pound almond, pecan, or walnut meats

• Sift sugar and spices together 3 times. Spread one half of the mixture, ¼ inch thick, on baking sheet or shallow pan. Place egg white, honey, and salt in bowl, and beat until mixed but not foamy. Add nuts and stir until coated. Place nuts on sugar, one at a time, top side up, ¼ inch apart. Cover evenly with remaining sugar mixture. Set pan inside another baking sheet, or pan, and bake in very slow oven (250° F.) 1½ hours*. Remove nuts immediately and brush off excess sugar. Cool. Store in airtight glass jar. Approximate yield: 1 pound.

* A very slow oven is necessary to make nuts crisp and to prevent them from becoming too brown.

Honey Penuche

2 cups brown sugar

¼ teaspoon salt

⅔ cup white sugar

1 cup milk

¼ cup honey

3 tablespoons butter

½ cup chopped nuts

• Combine all ingredients except butter and nuts, and cook over a low flame to 240° F. Stir just enough to prevent sticking. Remove from fire, add butter, and cool to lukewarm. Do not stir. Beat until candy begins to thicken. Add nuts and turn into a greased shallow pan. When firm, cut into squares.

Cream Candy

1 cup sugar

¼ cup cream

¼ cup honey

1 tablespoon butter

½ cup chopped nuts

• Mix sugar, cream, and honey. Cook until the sugar is dissolved. Add butter and continue without stirring until a very soft-ball stage is reached (236° F.). Remove from fire and begin to beat at once. Beat until thick and dull in appearance. Add nuts just before turning out. Pour into greased pan. Cut with a warm knife before the mixture is cold.

Honey Popcorn Balls

¾ cup sugar

1 teaspoon salt

½ cup water

¾ cup honey

3 quarts popcorn

• Cook sugar, salt, and water (stir until sugar is dissolved) to very brittle stage (300° F.). Add honey slowly, stirring until blended. Cook again until thermometer registers 240° F. (about one minute). Pour over popcorn and form into balls. Wrap in heavy waxed paper.

Fruit Candy

¼ cup dried prunes
¼ cup dried apricots
¼ cup dried figs
½ cup dates
¼ cup raisins
⅓ cup honey

• Let cleaned dried prunes and apricots stand in boiling water for five minutes. Run all the fruit through a food chopper, fine knife. Add honey. With buttered hands shape into balls. Roll in chopped nuts, cocoanut, or coat with confectioners' chocolate. Nuts may be added and other dried fruits like peaches and pears used.

Honeyed Fruit Strips

Orange peel
water
salt
honey

• Remove peel from 3 oranges; cut peel into strips. Cover with water to which 1 teaspoon of salt has been added. Boil 30 minutes; drain; cover with fresh water; boil until peel is tender. Drain. Add honey enough to cover, from ¾ to 1 cup. Let *simmer very slowly* until peel is clear (about 45 minutes). Lay on waxed paper and let stand 2 or 3 days before using.

Variations: Grapefruit peel and lemon peel may be similarly prepared.
Fruit strips may be rolled in cocoanut or nuts and used as a confection.
Peel may be coated with confectioners' chocolate.
Peel may be chopped and used in cookies, nut bread, muffin mixtures.

Honey Twists

½ cup honey
1 cup sugar
½ cup milk
¼ teaspoon salt
1 teaspoon vanilla extract

• Combine ingredients and cook over a low heat until when tested a hard ball is formed in cold water (260° F.). Stir occasionally. Pour into a shallow greased pan. Pull until light and firm as soon as it is cool enough to handle. Twist into rope form and cut in one or two-inch lengths. Wrap in waxed paper and store in a cool place.

Honey Marshmallows

1 tablespoon gelatine
¼ cup cold water
1 cup honey
¾ to 1 pound cocoanut

• Soak gelatin well in cold water. Dissolve gelatin over hot water and add to the honey which has been warmed. Beat until very light and fluffy (about 10 minutes by machine, and 20 minutes by hand). Turn out on oiled pan and let stand 24 to 48 hours. Toast cocoanut and roll to make fine. Spread cocoanut over the surface of a large pan and turn the marshmallows on it. Dip knife into cold water and cut into squares. Roll each piece in the cocoanut.

Nougat

¾ cup honey
1 cup sugar
¼ teaspoon salt
½ cup water
2 egg whites
1 teaspoon flavoring
¾ cup chopped nuts

● Combine honey, sugar, salt, and water and cook over low heat. Stir until sugar is dissolved and mixture starts to boil. Boil without stirring to 300° F. Pour hot sirup slowly over stiffly-beaten egg whites, beating constantly. Fold in nuts and flavoring. Spread in greased square pan. Cool and cut in rectangular pieces.

Peanut Brittle

2 cups sugar
1 cup honey
1 cup water
2 cups salted peanuts
1 tablespoon butter

● Put sugar, honey, water in sauce pan. Stir until sugar is dissolved. Cook to 300° F. Remove from fire. Add butter and peanuts. Stir just enough to mix thoroughly. Pour into very thin sheets on a well-greased platter. Cool. Break into pieces to serve.

Honey Squares

¼ cup honey
2 cups sugar
3 tablespoons water
¼ teaspoon salt
1 cup nut meats, broken
1 teaspoon flavoring

● Cook honey, sugar, water, and salt until soft-ball test is given. Take from fire. Add nuts and flavoring. Beat until creamy. Pour on buttered pan. Cut into squares.

Super Delicious Caramels

1½ cups thin cream
2 cups sugar
¼ cup butter
1 cup honey
½ teaspoon vanilla extract
1 cup nut meats

● Cook first four ingredients over low heat to 254° F., or hard-ball stage, stirring constantly toward the end of the cooking period. Add vanilla and nuts. Pour into buttered pan. Cut when cold and wrap each in oiled paper.

Candy Roll

½ pound sweet chocolate
(cooking)
3 tablespoons honey
¼ teaspoon salt
3 teaspoons cold water
1 cup peanut butter
3 tablespoons honey

● Melt chocolate in top of double boiler over hot water (not boiling). Add honey and salt. Stir until smooth. Add water, about one teaspoon at a time, beating well after each addition. Beat until smooth and shiny.

Pour mixture on sheet of heavy waxed paper. Spread into rectangular shape. Let stand for 10 to 15 minutes. Blend peanut butter and the 3 tablespoons honey and spread on chocolate. Roll up like jelly roll. Wrap well in waxed paper and place in refrigerator over night. Cut in slices to serve.

25

CONFITURES

*"A little honey in the canning
Mixed with the juices is good planning."*

- Use a large kettle when making jelly or jams in which part or all honey is used.
  Since honey contains some moisture, it is necessary to cook the mixture somewhat longer in order to obtain the desired consistency.

Currant Jelly

- Pick over currants. Do not remove stems. Wash. Drain. Place in preserving kettle. Mash with potato masher. Add ½ cup water to about 2 quarts fruit. Bring to a boil, simmer until currants appear white. Strain through a jelly bag. Measure juice. Add ¾ cup honey and ¾ cup sugar to 2 cups juice. Cook only 4 cupfuls of juice at a time. Stir until sugar dissolves. Cook until two drops run together and "sheet" off spoon. Fill hot, sterilized glasses. Cover with paraffin.

Rhubarb Jelly

1 cup rhubarb juice
2 tablespoons granulated pectin
1 cup honey

- Wash and cut rhubarb into inch lengths. Place in preserving kettle. Add enough water to prevent it from sticking. Cook slowly in covered kettle until soft. Strain in jelly bag. Measure juice. Add pectin and stir vigorously. Bring to a boil. Add honey and continue to boil until jelly test is secured. Fill hot, sterilized glasses with jelly. Cover with paraffin.

Sunshine Preserves

1½ cups honey
1½ cups sugar
1   quart pitted cherries

- Combine honey and sugar. Bring slowly to the boiling point, add cherries and cook 12 minutes. Pour out on shallow dishes; cover with glass and allow to stand in the sunshine one day or longer. Seal in hot, sterilized glasses.

Sweet Fruit Pickles

2 cups honey
1 cup vinegar
2 inches stick cinnamon
6 whole cloves
  apples

• Combine honey, vinegar, and spices, and heat to boiling. Have ready 8 to 10 cups of quartered apples (pared or not, as you like). Cook 2 or 3 cups of apples at a time in the sirup, handling them gently so they will not mash. When transparent, lift out and place in a jar or bowl, and continue until all are cooked. Take out spices, pour remaining sirup over the apples, and store in sterilized jars until needed. Serve cold with meats.

Honey Chutney

2 quarts sour apples
2 green peppers
3 onions, medium
¾ pound seedless raisins
½ tablespoon salt
1 cup honey
  Juice of 2 lemons and the grated rind of 1
1½ cups vinegar
¾ cup tart fruit juice
¾ tablespoon ginger
¼ teaspoon cayenne pepper

• Wash and chop fruit and vegetables. Add all other ingredients and simmer until thick like Chili Sauce. Seal in hot, sterilized jars.

Honey Orange Marmalade

2 oranges, medium
¼ grapefruit, medium
⅛ lemon
4¾ cups water per pound of fruit
¾ pound sugar per pound of fruit and liquid
¼ pound honey per pound of fruit and liquid

• Cut the fruit into very thin slices, cut each slice into eighths, remove the seeds, the pithy inner portion, and about ½ of the orange rind. Add the water to the fruit and let stand in the refrigerator 24 hours. Remove. Boil steadily for about 1 hour, or until the rind is tender and slightly translucent. Weigh the fruit and liquid and add the required amount of sugar. Boil slowly until it reaches 214° F., add the required amount of honey, and cook to 218° F. Remove from stove and seal in sterilized glasses. Yield: Approximately one quart.

Canned Peaches

3 cups water
½ cup sugar
½ cup honey
12 peaches

• Prepare sirup by boiling water and sugar for 5 minutes. Add honey. Scald peaches in boiling water to loosen skins; peel, cut in halves and remove stones. Cook fruit in sirup. Allow 1 peach stone to 6 peaches. Cook from 5 to 10 minutes. Test by piercing with silver fork. Arrange peaches when done with cut side down in jar. Fill to overflowing with hot sirup and remove air bubbles with sterilized knife. Cover with lid just taken from boiling water. Note: Pears may be canned in the same way.

COOKIES

*"Of all the cookies I have eaten
Those made with honey can't be beaten."*

Everyday Cookies

½ cup shortening
½ cup sugar
½ cup honey
1   egg
⅔ cup flour
½ teaspoon soda
½ teaspoon baking powder
¼ teaspoon salt
1   cup quick cooking oats
1   cup shredded cocoanut
1   teaspoon vanilla extract
½ cup chopped nut meats

• Cream shortening, sugar, and honey together until light and fluffy. Add well-beaten egg, blend together. Sift flour with dry ingredients; stir well. Add oats, cocoanut, and vanilla. Add nut meats. Spread on greased baking sheets; bake in moderate oven (350° F.). Bake about 12 to 15 minutes. Cut into bars.

Fig Newtons

1   cup honey
1   cup shortening
1   cup sugar
2   eggs
    juice and rind of ½ lemon
6½ cups flour
2   teaspoons baking powder
1   teaspoon soda
1   teaspoon salt

• Cream honey, shortening, and sugar. Add beaten eggs, lemon juice, and rind. Add flour which has been sifted three times with baking powder, salt, and soda. Roll dough quite thin, cut into strips about 6 inches long and 3 inches wide. Put filling in center of the strip, and lap sides over. Bake 15 minutes, 400° F. Cool. Cut into desired size, crosswise.

Fig Filling

4 cups ground figs
1 cup honey and ¼ cup water
  juice of ½ lemon and
    ½ orange

• Combine and cook 15 minutes, stirring constantly. Cool before using.

28

Hermits

½ cup shortening
1 cup honey
½ cup brown sugar
2 eggs, well beaten
3 tablespoons milk
2¼ cups flour
1 teaspoon baking soda
½ teaspoon cinnamon
½ teaspoon allspice
1 cup seedless raisins
1 cup currants
1 cup dates
½ cup nuts

● Cream shortening, add honey and sugar, well-beaten eggs, milk and dry ingredients, fruit and nuts. Drop from teaspoon upon a greased cooky sheet. Bake at 400° F. for 10 to 12 minutes. Makes about 7¾ dozen.

Chocolate Chip Cookies

½ cup shortening
½ cup honey
1 small egg
1 cup sifted flour
1 teaspoon baking powder
¼ teaspoon salt
½ teaspoon vanilla extract
½ cup semi-sweet chocolate chips
¼ cup nut meats chopped

● Cream shortening and honey until light and fluffy. Add egg and beat well. Sift flour, baking powder, and salt twice. Add flour mixture to shortening mixture; add vanilla and blend all well. Fold in chocolate chips and nuts. Chill and drop by teaspoonfuls on greased cooky sheet. Bake at 375° F. for 12 minutes.

All Honey Cookies

1 cup honey
1 cup shortening
3¾ cups flour
4⅝ teaspoons baking powder
⅛ teaspoon soda
½ teaspoon each cinnamon, cloves, and allspice

● Heat honey and shortening together about 1 minute. Cool. Sift flour, baking powder, soda, and spices together. Add flour to first mixture to make a soft dough. Roll thin, cut, bake at 350° F. for 12 to 15 minutes.

Honey Pecan Cookies

½ cup shortening
1 cup honey
1 egg
¼ cup sour milk
2 cups flour
½ teaspoon soda
½ teaspoon salt
¾ cup pecans
¾ cup each of raisins, cherries, and dates

● Cream shortening and honey; add the egg, sour milk, and flour which has been sifted with soda and salt. Add the nuts and fruit. Drop on greased pans and bake at 350° F. for 15 minutes.

29

Pecan Butterballs

1 cup butter
¼ cup honey
2 cups sifted flour
½ teaspoon salt
2 teaspoons vanilla extract
2 cups finely chopped pecans

• Cream butter; add honey gradually; add flour, salt and vanilla. Mix well and add chopped nuts. Form into very small balls on a greased baking sheet and bake in a moderate oven (300° F.) for 40 to 45 minutes. Roll in powdered sugar while still hot. Cool, roll again in the powdered sugar.

Raisin Honey Gems

1½ cups honey
¾ cup shortening
1 egg, beaten
2½ cups flour
¼ teaspoon salt
¼ teaspoon soda
2¼ teaspoons baking powder
1 teaspoon cinnamon
1½ cups oatmeal (uncooked)
¾ cup raisins
2 tablespoons hot water

• Cream honey and shortening. Add beaten egg. Sift flour, salt, soda, baking powder, and cinnamon into mixture. Add oatmeal, raisins, and water. Mix thoroughly. Drop by teaspoonfuls upon greased cooky sheet. Bake in moderate oven (375° F.) for 15 minutes.

Butter Cookies

1 pound butter
1 cup honey
2 eggs
   grated rind of ½ lemon
8 cups flour
1¼ teaspoons baking powder
   juice of ½ lemon
1 cup almonds, chopped

• Cream butter, add the honey, yolks of eggs, slightly beaten; add grated rind of lemon and flour mixed with baking powder. Add lemon juice. Chill dough. The dough may be formed into small balls, rolled and cut. Brush with the white of egg and sprinkle the chopped almonds on top. Bake at 350° F. 10 to 15 minutes. (Will keep well.)

Variations

• Divide dough into 8 parts. Use coloring liquid. Color one part red, another blue, one green, and one yellow. Add ½ ounce melted chocolate to one part. Keep one part natural color. Add ¼ teaspoon cinnamon, ¼ teaspoon nutmeg to one part, and any combination of fruit (dates or raisins) and chopped nuts to the last part. Many different shapes and combinations will suggest themselves; for example, roll red dough ⅛ inch thick into a rectangle, roll the green the same thickness and size. Place on top of red. Roll as for a jelly roll. Chill, cut into thin slices. Bake.

Honey Nut Brownies

¼ cup shortening
2 squares chocolate
½ cup honey
1 teaspoon vanilla extract
½ cup sugar
2 eggs
½ cup flour (sifted with ¼ teaspoon baking powder)
¼ teaspoon salt
1 cup chopped nuts

• Melt shortening and chocolate together. Add honey, vanilla, sugar, and beaten eggs. Sift flour, baking powder, and salt and add nuts. Add this to first mixture. Bake in a shallow pan which has been lined with well greased waxed paper, in a slow oven (300° F.) for 45 minutes.

Honey Peanut Rocks

1 cup shortening
½ cup brown sugar
½ cup honey
2 cups flour
2½ teaspoons baking powder
⅒ teaspoon soda
⅓ cup milk
2 cups quick-cooking oatmeal
1 cup each of chopped raisins and peanuts

• Cream shortening. Add brown sugar and honey gradually and cream well. Add flour sifted with baking powder and soda alternately with milk. Add the oatmeal, raisins, and peanuts. Drop from a teaspoon upon a greased cooky sheet. Bake in a slow oven (300° F.) 15 to 20 minutes.

Honey Bars

1 cup honey
3 eggs, well beaten
1 teaspoon baking powder
1⅛ cups flour
1 cup chopped nuts
1 pound chopped dates
1 teaspoon vanilla extract

• Mix honey and well-beaten eggs together. Add baking powder and flour sifted together, chopped nuts, dates, and extract. Bake in a long, flat pan. Mixture should be ¼ inch deep, and ½ inch after baking. Cut into strips ½ inch wide and 3 inches long. Before serving roll in powdered sugar. These are fine for the holidays since they can be made ahead of time and will improve in flavor. (Bake at 350° F. for 15 to 20 minutes.)

Honey Gingernuts

1 cup honey
1 cup sugar
1 cup softened shortening
1 egg, beaten
2 cups flour
2 teaspoons baking powder
3 teaspoons ginger
1 cup chopped nuts
additional flour

• Mix honey, sugar, shortening, and egg. Sift flour, baking powder, and ginger. Combine flour mixture with honey mixture. Add nuts. Add more flour, enough to make batter of right consistency. Drop by teaspoonfuls upon a greased cooky sheet and bake at 350° to 375° F.

Christmas Fruit Nuggets

1 cup shortening
1½ cups honey
2 eggs
3 cups sifted cake flour
3 teaspoons baking powder
¼ teaspoon salt
½ teaspoon each cloves, cinnamon, and nutmeg
½ cup milk
½ cup candied pineapple
1 cup candied cherries
1 cup candied raisins
1 cup English walnuts

• Cream shortening. Add honey and cream together. Beat eggs and add. Sift together cake flour, baking powder, salt, cloves, cinnamon, nutmeg, and add alternately with milk. Chop pineapple, cherries, raisins, and walnuts. Mix all together well. Drop by teaspoonfuls either upon greased baking pan or into tiny paper cups. Bake in moderate oven (375° F.) for about 15 minutes.

Lebkucken

4 eggs
¼ pound sugar
¼ pound honey
½ pound flour
2 teaspoons soda
3 teaspoons cinnamon
½ teaspoon cardamon
½ teaspoon cloves
⅛ pound orange peel
¼ pound citron
  grated rind of ½ lemon
¼ pound shelled almonds

• Beat whole eggs until very light, add sugar and honey and sifted dry ingredients. Beat well. Add fruits and nuts. Bake in moderate oven (350° F.) in two 10 x 16-inch pans. Ice with powdered sugar and cream.

Christmas Cookies

2 cups brown sugar
½ cup honey
¼ cup shortening
1 egg
2½ cups flour
3 teaspoons baking powder
1 teaspoon cinnamon
2 ounces of citron, ground very fine
  juice of ½ orange and grated rind and juice of ½ lemon
½ cup almonds, blanched and chopped

• Cook sugar and honey until sugar is dissolved. Add shortening and cool. Add beaten egg. Sift the dry ingredients and add to the sirup. Add chopped fruit, fruit juices, and nuts. If necessary, add just a bit more flour to handle it easily. Roll ⅛ inch thick and cut into fancy shapes. Bake on greased cooky sheet at 350° F. for 10 minutes.

Honey Nut Cookies

2 egg whites
½ cup honey
½ cup sugar
¼ teaspoon salt
¼ cup water
1 tablespoon flavoring
1 cup chopped black walnuts

● Beat egg whites with rotary beater until stiff. Gradually add honey, beating after each addition. Continue beating until mixture is stiff. Combine sugar, salt, and water in small saucepan. Cook until sugar is dissolved and mixture boils, stirring constantly. Cover tightly and boil 2 minutes. Uncover and boil, without stirring, until a small amount of sirup forms a firm ball in cold water (250° F.). Pour sirup in fine stream over egg mixture, beating constantly. Beat until cool and thickened. Add flavoring and nuts. Drop from teaspoon upon well-buttered, floured baking sheet. Bake in slow oven (300° F.) 25 to 30 minutes, or until delicately browned. Carefully remove from sheet with sharp edge of clean knife. Store in tightly covered jar with waxed paper between each layer. Approximate yield: 5 dozen cookies.

Honey Oatmeal Cookies

½ cup shortening
1 cup honey
1 egg
1½ cups sifted flour
½ teaspoon soda
½ teaspoon salt
1⅝ cups oatmeal
4 tablespoons sour milk
½ cup chopped peanuts
1 cup raisins

● Cream shortening. Add the honey and blend. Stir in the egg. Sift together dry ingredients and add oatmeal. Add dry ingredients alternately with milk to shortening and honey mixture. Stir in nuts and raisins. Drop by spoonful upon a greased pan or baking sheet. Bake in a moderate oven (350° F.) for 15 minutes. Yield: 3 dozen cookies.

Honey Peanut Butter Cookies

½ cup shortening
½ cup honey
½ cup brown sugar
1 egg
½ cup peanut butter
½ teaspoon salt
1¼ cups flour
½ teaspoon soda

● Cream shortening, honey, and sugar together until light and fluffy. Add well-beaten egg. Add peanut butter and salt. Stir in flour and soda sifted together and mix well. Form into small balls of dough. Place upon greased cooky sheet. Press with a fork. Bake in moderate oven (350° F.) 12 to 15 minutes.

Christmas Honey-Ginger Cookies

2 cups sifted flour
⅛ teaspoon soda
⅓ cup honey
½ teaspoon ground ginger
½ teaspoon salt
½ cup sugar
2 tablespoons water
1 egg, slightly beaten
1 teaspoon orange extract
½ cup chopped crystallized ginger
½ cup chopped blanched almonds

● Sift flour once, measure, add soda and sift again. Place honey, ground ginger, salt, sugar, water, egg, and orange extract in bowl, and beat with rotary beater until well blended. Add crystallized ginger and nuts, mixing thoroughly. Stir in flour. Chill thoroughly. Place on lightly-floured board, roll ¼ inch thick, and cut into fancy Christmas shapes. Brush cookies with egg, and sprinkle with colored sugar or tiny Christmas candy mixtures. Bake on ungreased baking sheet in moderately slow oven (325° F.) 12 to 15 minutes. Cool. Store in airtight container. Approximate yield: 5 dozen (2½-inch) cookies.

33

Peanut Butter Brownies

¼ cup shortening
2 tablespoons peanut butter
3 tablespoons cocoa
½ cup sugar
1 egg
½ cup honey
¾ cup sifted flour
½ teaspoon baking powder
¼ teaspoon salt
½ cup nut meats

• Cream shortening and peanut butter together. Add cocoa and sugar (sifted together) a little at a time. Cream well. Add egg and beat well. Add honey a little at a time and beat until well blended. Add baking powder, salt, and flour sifted together. Add nut meats. Mix well. Spread mixture in well-greased 8 x 8-inch pan. Bake in moderate oven (350° F.) for 35 minutes. Cut into 1 or 2-inch squares for serving.

Date Peanut Butter Drops

½ cup shortening
¾ cup peanut butter
½ cup sugar
½ cup honey
1 teaspoon vanilla extract
2 eggs
1 cup chopped dates
2 cups sifted enriched flour
2½ teaspoons baking powder
½ teaspoon salt
¼ cup milk

• Cream together shortening, peanut butter, and sugar. Add honey and beat. Blend in vanilla extract. Beat eggs and add. Add dates. Sift together flour, baking powder, and salt, and add to creamed mixture alternately with milk. Blend well. Drop by teaspoonfuls on greased baking sheet and bake in moderate oven (350° F.) 15 minutes. Yield: 4 dozen 2-inch cookies.

Honey Jam Bars

½ cup shortening
½ cup honey
1½ cups sifted flour
1 teaspoon baking powder
½ teaspoon salt
1 teaspoon cinnamon
¼ teaspoon nutmeg
¼ teaspoon allspice
1 egg, beaten
¾ cup jam

• Cream shortening. Add honey. Blend well. Add sifted dry ingredients and mix. Add beaten egg. Spread half batter in greased pan and spread with jam. Cover jam with rest of batter. Bake in hot oven (400° F.) 30 to 35 minutes. Cut into 1 x 4-inch bars. Yield: 2 dozen bars.

Eggless Honey Cookies

½ cup honey
½ cup shortening
2 cups flour
½ teaspoon cinnamon
½ teaspoon cloves
1 teaspoon soda

• Heat honey and shortening carefully for a minute or two. When cool add dry ingredients that have been sifted together several times. Roll out to ¼ inch in thickness and cut with a doughnut cutter. Bake on greased cooky sheet for 12 to 15 minutes in a moderate oven (350° F.). When cold frost with a powdered sugar frosting. Decorate with clusters of red cinnamon candies and bits of green gum drops to form holly wreath design.

Chocolate Fruit Cookies

½ cup honey
½ cup sugar
½ cup melted shortening
2 eggs
3 squares chocolate, melted
1 teaspoon soda
½ cup milk
2 cups flour
1 cup raisins and nuts (dates may be used)
1 teaspoon vanilla extract

• Add honey and sugar to melted shortening. Add the yolks of eggs and beat well. Add melted chocolate. Add soda to milk and then add milk and ½ the flour alternately. Mix well. Add raisins and nuts with remainder of flour. Add beaten whites of eggs and extract. Drop from teaspoon on buttered baking sheet. Bake 10 to 15 minutes at 350° F.

Honey Peanut Cookies

1 cup shortening
½ cup honey
½ cup brown sugar
⅓ cup milk
2 cups flour
1 teaspoon soda
1 teaspoon baking powder
2 cups quick-cooking oats
1 cup raisins, chopped
1 cup peanuts, chopped

• Cream the shortening, add the honey, brown sugar, and the rest of the ingredients in the order given. Roll a teaspoonful of the dough in the hands, place on an ungreased cooky sheet, flattening a little. Bake in a slow oven (325° F.) for 15 to 20 minutes. Yield: 4 to 5 dozen cookies.

Chocolate Pecan Squares

⅔ cup flour
½ teaspoon baking powder
½ teaspoon salt
⅓ cup shortening
2 squares chocolate
½ cup sugar
2 eggs, well beaten
½ cup honey
½ cup broken pecan meats
1 teaspoon vanilla extract

• Sift flour, baking powder, and salt together. Melt shortening and chocolate together over boiling water. Add sugar to eggs and beat well. Add honey gradually and beat thoroughly. Add shortening and chocolate mixture and beat well. Add dry ingredients, nuts, and vanilla. Place whole pecans on batter in pan before baking. Bake in greased 8 x 8 x 2-inch pans in moderate oven (350° F.) about 40 minutes. When done, cut into squares so that a pecan meat will be in center of each square.

Honey Cakes

3 pounds honey
1½ pounds sugar
2½ pounds flour
½ pound citron
1 tablespoon cinnamon
1 tablespoon cloves
1 teaspoon cardamon
1 nutmeg, grated
7 eggs
1 pound flour
1¼ pounds almonds
2 lemons, juice and rind
1 teaspoon baking powder (optional)

• Heat honey and sugar together over low heat until sugar is dissolved. Add the flour. Remove from heat. Add the citron, cut very fine, and spices. Add beaten eggs and the one pound of flour. Add almonds, which have been ground and roasted in the oven with a little sugar until light brown. Add lemon juice and rind. Mix well. Chill dough for several days before baking. Roll dough ¼ inch thick and cut with Christmas cooky cutters. ake at 350° F. 12–15 minutes. Ice with a thin icing. Use rosewater for flavoring. The cookies should be made a month before using. Cookies keep well in a stone crock.

35

D E S S E R T S

"If you a happy cook would be,
Use honey in your recipe."

Honeyed Apples and Cranberries

6   medium-sized apples
½ lb. (2¼ cups) cranberries
1¾ cups water
½ cup honey
1½ cups sugar
¼ teaspoon salt
2   cinnamon sticks

• Pare and core apples and place in flat-bottomed pan. Add cranberries and water and simmer 5 minutes, turning apples once during cooking period. Add remaining ingredients. Simmer 15 to 20 minutes longer, or until apples are tender. (Turn apples carefully during cooking so they are evenly red.) Remove apples to dish in which they are to be served, skim the cranberry sauce, and pour around apples. Cool. Cover tightly and place in refrigerator until ready to use. Approximate yield: 8–10 portions.

Honey Baked Pears

8   pear halves
¼ cup lemon juice
½ cup honey
1   teaspoon cinnamon
2   tablespoons butter

• Arrange pears in shallow buttered baking dish. Pour over the lemon juice and honey. Sprinkle with cinnamon and dot with butter. Bake in moderate oven at 350° F. Serve hot with cream as dessert. Peaches prepared this way make a delicious dessert.

Broiled Grapefruit

• Wash and dry the grapefruit and cut in half crosswise allowing one half to each person. With a sharp knife cut around and under the entire pulp being careful to leave all the membrane in the shell. Cut down on each side of each section loosening each section completely. Now with two fingers lift out the center core, to which will be attached the radiating membranes. This leaves the shell containing only the nicely separated fruit section. Spread the top of each half with honey and dot with butter. Place under the broiler flame or in a moderate oven until the honey begins to carmelize and the ingredients are well blended. Serve hot as dessert or a first course.

Baked Apple with Honey Filling

• Wash and core the apples. Leave part of the core in the bottom of the apples to act as a plug. Fill the cavity with honey, using as much as the tartness of the apples requires. For variety, add a bit of lemon juice, or a few cinnamon candies. One may stuff the cavity with raisins and dates or other fruit combinations.

Honey Apple Crisp

4 cups sliced apples	• Spread sliced apples in a shallow baking dish,
1/4 cup sugar	sprinkle with sugar and lemon juice and pour
1 tablespoon lemon juice	honey over all. In a bowl mix flour, brown sugar,
1/2 cup honey	and salt, and work in the butter as for biscuits,
1/2 cup flour	making a crumbly mixture. Spread these crumbs
1/4 cup brown sugar	evenly over the apples and bake in a moderate
1/4 teaspoon salt	oven (375° F.) for 30 to 40 minutes, or until
1/4 cup butter	apples are tender and crust crisply browned. Serve
1/4 cup walnuts (if desired)	warm, with plain cream, or whipped cream
	topped with a dash of powdered cinnamon.

Marguerites

• Place salted crackers in a baking pan. Spread crackers with honey and chopped nuts. Place in oven until slightly browned.

Ice Cream Sundae

• Pour honey over ice cream, sprinkle nuts on top or garnish with a cherry. This is a delicious and nutritious dessert.

Honey Ice Cream

2 cups milk	• Scald 2 cups whole milk, add honey and salt.
3/4 cup honey	Beat eggs. Pour scalded milk into the egg mix-
1/4 teaspoon salt	ture and stir until well blended. Return to double
2 eggs	boiler and cook for three or four minutes. Cool.
1 cup cream	Beat cream and fold into custard mixture. Freeze
	in refrigerator. Stir once or twice while freezing.

Honey Peppermint Ice Cream (Freezer)

1½ teaspoons gelatin	• Soak gelatin in cold water. Heat milk and
2 tablespoons water	cream and add honey; mix well. Add gelatin
1/2 cup milk	slowly, stirring constantly to prevent lumping.
2½ cups coffee cream	(Thoroughly chill if you wish to shorten freez-
1/8 cup honey	ing time.) Pour in freezer with crushed candy
3/4 cup crushed peppermint stick candy	and freeze, or if bits of the candy are desired in the ice cream, add it after the mix has become semi-solid. Unsweetened chocolate (1 square) cut into very small pieces may be added. (A good proportion of salt and ice to use is 1 part of salt to 4 of ice.)

Pastry

1½ cups flour

½ teaspoon baking powder (optional)

½ teaspoon salt

½ cup lard or other shortening

about 4 tablespoons cold water

● Sift dry ingredients. Cut or work in the shortening, leaving some of the shortening in pieces the size of a pea, and add enough cold water to hold ingredients together. Toss on a floured board and roll out carefully. This makes two crusts.

Apple Pie

6 medium sized apples (or 3 cups sliced apples)

1 tablespoon butter

1 cup honey

2 tablespoons lemon juice

● Quarter and pare apples, remove core and slice. Line a 9-inch pie plate with pastry. Place the sliced apples on this. Dot with bits of butter and add a perforated upper crust, pushing it toward the center. Press edges together and trim. Bake in a hot oven (450° F.) for ten minutes; then about 30 minutes at 350° F., or until the crust is slightly browned and the fruit is soft. Remove from oven, add honey which has been mixed with lemon juice, carefully through the perforations in top crust. By the time the pie is ready to serve the honey will have been absorbed by the apples.

Honey Raisin Pie

1½ cups raisins

1 tablespoon grated orange rind

1 cup orange juice

4 tablespoons lemon juice

¾ cup honey

2 tablespoons butter

½ teaspoon salt

4 tablespoons cornstarch

¾ cup cold water

pastry for double crust (9-inch)

● Rinse and drain raisins. Combine with orange rind and juice, lemon juice, honey, butter, salt, and cornstarch that has been moistened in the cold water, and stir until blended. Bring to a boil and cook and stir until mixture thickens (about 3 or 4 minutes). Pour into pastry-lined pie pan, cover with top crust. Bake in a moderately hot oven (425° F.) 30 to 35 minutes. Cool before serving. Serves 6 to 8.

Pumpkin Pie

2 cups stewed pumpkin

2 cups rich milk

1 cup honey

2 eggs

½ teaspoon salt

1 teaspoon cinnamon

½ teaspoon ginger

● Mix ingredients in order given. Beat well. Pour into pastry-lined pie pan. Bake in moderate oven (350° F.) 1 hour.

For variation, replace water with orange juice in pastry recipe.

For a festive note, add pastry turkey or pumpkin designs. Roll pastry thin. Cut out, using cardboard or metal pattern. Bake on cooky sheet. When done, place on top of pie.

Peach Pie

Peaches

1 tablespoon quick cooking tapioca

½ cup honey

● Line pie pan with pastry. Fill with sliced fresh peaches. Sprinkle with tapioca. Pour honey over peaches. Cover with strips of pastry. Bake in hot oven (425° F.) about 40 minutes.

Pecan Pie

½ cup honey
½ cup brown sugar
¼ cup butter
3 eggs, beaten
1 cup pecan meats

● Blend honey and sugar together. Cook slowly to form a smooth sirup. Add butter. Add beaten eggs and broken pecan meats. Pour into pie pan lined with pastry. Bake in moderate oven (400° F.) 10 minutes. Reduce temperature to 350° F. and bake for 30 minutes, or until mixture sets.

Chiffon Pie

1 tablespoon gelatin
¼ cup cold water
3 egg yolks
½ cup honey
¼ cup orange juice
3 tablespoons lemon juice
3 egg whites

● Soak gelatin in cold water. Place egg yolks and honey in top of double boiler. Stir well. Add orange and lemon juices. Cook slowly over hot water stirring constantly until thickened. Add gelatin and stir until dissolved. Remove from heat. Chill. When mixture begins to settle, fold in the stiffly-beaten egg whites. Pour into baked pastry shell. Chill.

Deep Dish Apple Pie

● Wash and quarter apples. Pare. Cut into thin slices. Fill deep pie plate with apple slices. Pour 1 cup honey to which 1 tablespoon lemon juice has been added over apples. Sprinkle with cinnamon. Dot with butter. Cover with pastry. Prick design in crust to allow steam to escape and for decoration. Bake in moderately hot oven (400° F.) about 40 minutes.

Berry Pie

3 cups berries
¾ to 1 cup honey
2 tablespoons cornstarch or
  4 tablespoons flour
½ teaspoon cinnamon
1 tablespoon butter

● Pick over and wash berries. Place in pastry-lined pie pan. Add a little honey to cornstarch. Blend well. Add remainder of honey. Pour over berries. Add a dash of cinnamon and dot with bits of butter. Cover with criss-cross pastry. Bake in hot oven (450° F.) 10 minutes. Reduce heat to 350° F. and bake 30 minutes.

Pumpkin Chiffon Pie

¼ cup cold water
1¼ cups pumpkin
½ cup honey
3 eggs, separated
½ cup milk
½ teaspoon ginger
1 teaspoon cinnamon
½ teaspoon nutmeg
¼ teaspoon salt
½ cup sugar

● Soak gelatin in water. To the pumpkin add honey, egg yolks beaten, milk, spices, and salt. Beat well. Cook over boiling water until mixture thickens. Add softened gelatin. Stir well. Chill until partially set. Add egg whites beaten with sugar. Pour into baked pastry shell. Chill. Serve with a spoonful of Honey Meringue.

Honey Delight

1 package lemon or orange
   flavored gelatin
½ cup boiling water
½ cup honey
   juice of ½ lemon
1 can evaporated milk
½ pound vanilla wafers

• Dissolve gelatin in boiling water. Add honey and lemon juice and mix well. Fold in the evaporated milk that has been chilled and whipped. Pour this mixture into a pan that has been lined with crushed vanilla wafers. Place crushed vanilla wafers on top of mixture and put in refrigerator to set. Cut into squares. Serves 6.

Fruit Rice Ring

3   tablespoons cornstarch
½   teaspoon salt
2   eggs
1½ cups milk
1   tablespoon butter
¼   cup honey
2   cups cooked rice

• Put cornstarch and salt in top of double boiler. Add egg yolks and milk. Stir well. Cook over boiling water, stirring constantly until mixture thickens. Remove from heat. Add butter, honey, and rice. Fold in beaten whites of eggs. Turn into buttered ring mold. Bake in moderate oven (350° F.) 30 minutes. Cool. Unmold carefully. Fill center with fruit.

Honey Custard

¼ teaspoon salt
3 eggs, slightly beaten
¼ cup honey
2 cups milk, scalded
   nutmeg

• Add salt to eggs. Beat eggs just long enough to combine whites and yolks. Add honey to milk. Add honey and milk mixture slowly to eggs. Pour into custard cups. Top with a few gratings of nutmeg. Set custard cups in pan of hot water. Bake in moderate oven (325° F.) about 40 minutes, or until custard is firm.

American Pudding

¾   cup sifted flour
1   teaspoon baking powder
½   teaspoon salt
4   tablespoons butter
⅓   cup sugar
½   cup milk
4   tablespoons currants
1½ teaspoons grated lemon
    rind
½   cup honey
1¼ cups boiling water

• Sift flour once, measure, add baking powder and salt, and sift again. Cream 2 tablespoons of the butter, add sugar gradually, creaming after each addition. Add 2 tablespoons of the milk and beat thoroughly. Add flour, alternately with remaining milk, a small amount at a time, beating after each addition until smooth. Add currants and lemon rind. Turn into well-greased baking dish, 8 x 8 x 2-inches. Combine remaining butter, honey, water, and dash of salt. Pour over batter. Bake in moderate oven (350° F.) 40 to 45 minutes. Serve warm with cream. Approximate yield: 6 portions.

Honey Hard Sauce

• Cream ⅓ cup butter and beat in gradually ¾ cup honey. Add 1 teaspoon lemon juice. Chill.

Honey Steamed Pudding

¼ cup butter
½ cup honey
1 egg, well beaten
2¼ cups sifted flour
3½ teaspoons baking powder
¼ teaspoon salt
1 cup milk
½ teaspoon vanilla extract

• Cream butter, add honey gradually and then the well beaten egg. Add the sifted dry ingredients and milk alternately. Add vanilla. Fill buttered individual molds ¾ full. Cover loosely with wax paper held in place with a rubber band. Place molds in a steamer for 30 minutes. Test with a toothpick. Serve hot. (Makes 12 molds).

Pudding Sauce

¼ cup sugar
6 tablespoons flour
½ cup honey
2 cups water
⅛ cup butter
   juice of 1 lemon and
      1 orange

• Mix sugar and flour, add honey and water. Cook in double boiler until thickened. Add butter and fruit juice. Serve hot.

Rice Pudding

2 cups cooked rice
3 cups milk
¾ cup honey
3 eggs
1 cup chopped raisins

• Mix rice, milk and honey. Add the eggs which have been slightly beaten. Stir in the chopped raisins. Bake at about 350° F. in a well-greased baking dish for about one hour. Serve with cream if desired. Serves 8.

Cranberry Pudding

2 cups large cranberries, cut in two and mixed with 1½ cups flour
⅔ cup honey
⅓ cup hot water
1 teaspoon soda
½ teaspoon salt
½ teaspoon baking powder

• Add dry ingredients to the cranberries mixed with the flour. Mix honey and hot water and add. Put in steamer and steam two hours. Serve with the following honey sauce.

Honey Sauce

½ cup butter
⅔ cup honey
2 tablespoons flour
2 eggs, slightly beaten
½ cup lemon juice
½ pint whipped cream

• Mix and cook first four ingredients slowly in double boiler until thickened. Remove from fire. Add lemon juice. When cool and ready to serve, fold in whipped cream.

French Apple Dumpling

2   cups flour
4   teaspoons baking powder
½   teaspoon salt
¼   cup lard
¾   cup milk
4   large apples
½   cup sugar
¼   teaspoon cinnamon
     melted butter

• Mix ingredients as for biscuit dough. Handle as lightly as possible. Roll out the dough on a floured towel one-fourth inch thick. Cover the dough with the sliced apples, and sprinkle over the apples the one-half cup sugar and the cinnamon. Roll like a jelly roll and cut into one-inch slices. (Makes 8 slices.) Place slices in a buttered baking pan. Put one teaspoon melted butter over each roll. Bake at 400° F, 20 to 25 minutes.

Honey Dumpling Sauce

1½   cups honey
2   tablespoons cornstarch
1½   cups water
⅛   teaspoon salt
1   tablespoon butter

• Mix the ingredients and cook until clear. Add ½ teaspoon vanilla. Serve on the hot slices.

Tart Pastry

2   cups flour
½   teaspoon salt
½   cup shortening
1   cup cottage cheese
3   tablespoons honey

• Sift dry ingredients and cut in shortening as for pie pastry. Add honey to the cheese. Add cheese to the flour mixture and blend with pastry cutter or knives. If cheese is not moist enough to make a good pastry, add a few drops of cold water. Roll thin on lightly-floured board.

Banbury Tarts

1   cup chopped raisins
¾   cup honey
3   tablespoons cracker crumbs
1   slightly beaten egg
1   tablespoon melted butter
⅛   teaspoon salt
½   lemon, juice and grated rind

• Combine all ingredients. Roll Tart Pastry thin and cut into three-inch squares. Place a teaspoon of Banbury mixture in the center of each square; cut edges, fold like a triangle and press edges together. Prick several times to allow steam to escape. Bake in hot oven (450° F.) for 15 minutes.

Coventry Tartlets

½   pound cottage or cream cheese
½   cup honey
¼   cup butter
2   egg yolks
½   teaspoon salt
¼   teaspoon nutmeg
1   tablespoon orange juice

• Combine all ingredients until of a creamy consistency. Line a dozen individual tart molds with Tart Pastry. Prick and fill with the cheese mixture. Bake in a hot oven (450° F.) for 10 minutes, reduce the heat to 325° F. and bake until golden brown and firm. Remove from the oven and cool. When ready to serve, garnish with red or green honey jelly.

42

Rhubarb Tarts

2 cups rhubarb
2 egg yolks
¾ cup honey
3 tablespoons flour
¼ teaspoon salt
2 egg whites
2 tablespoons honey

• Wash and cut rhubarb in ½-inch lengths. Pour boiling water over the rhubarb and drain in colander. Mix egg yolks slightly beaten, honey, flour, and salt. Add to rhubarb. Pour into pastry lined muffin pans. Bake in moderate oven (350° F.) 30 minutes or until done. Top with meringue made by adding 2 tablespoons honey to 2 stiffly-beaten egg whites.

Tapioca Cream

⅓ cup quick cooking tapioca
⅓ cup honey
¼ teaspoon salt
2 eggs
4 cups milk, scalded
1 teaspoon vanilla extract

• Combine tapioca, honey, salt, and egg yolks in top of double boiler. Add milk slowly and mix thoroughly. Cook until tapioca is transparent, stirring often. Remove from the heat and fold into the stiffly-beaten egg whites. Add the vanilla. This may be served either warm or cold with cream.

Rhubarb Brown Betty

2 cups bread crumbs
3 cups rhubarb cut in ½-inch pieces (apples may be used)
½ cup honey
¼ cup water
½ teaspoon nutmeg
3 tablespoons butter

• Mix ¾ of the bread crumbs and ¾ fruit and place in a deep baking dish. Bring honey and water to a boil. Pour over bread and fruit mixture. Sprinkle remainder of crumbs over this, sprinkle with nutmeg and dot with butter. Arrange the rest of the fruit so that each serving will have one or more pieces of fruit on top. Bake in moderate oven (315° F.) 30 to 40 minutes.

Honey Parfait

2 eggs, separated
pinch salt
½ cup honey
1 teaspoon vanilla extract
1⅝ cups evaporated milk, chilled

• Beat egg whites until foamy. Add honey gradually. Beat constantly. Add egg yolks and vanilla. Beat until well blended. Fold in stiffly beaten, chilled milk. Garnish with maraschino cherries. Pour into freezing trays. Serves 8.

Rhubarb Medley

3 cups rhubarb
1 cup honey
cinnamon candies
2 eggs
1 tablespoon gelatin

• Wash rhubarb and cut into pieces of about 1-inch in length. Place in sauce pan. Add 1 cup honey and enough water to prevent it from scorching. Cover and cook slowly until tender. During last five minutes add enough cinnamon candies to give it a deep pink color. Add a little of the hot mixture to 2 beaten egg yolks. Return to sauce pan. Soften 1 tablespoon of gelatin in a little cold water in large bowl. Gradually add hot mixture to this. Just before it begins to set, fold in the two egg whites that have been stiffly beaten. Pour into molds and chill. Serve with whipped cream.

M E A T S

"A drop or two of Nature's sweet
Will give a better taste to meat."

Baked Ham

1 ham
1 cup honey
cloves

• Select a good quality ham. Wipe meat with a damp cloth and remove unsightly parts. Place ham fat side up in roasting pan. Add no water. Bake uncovered in slow oven (300° F.). Insert a meat thermometer with the bulb at the center of the largest muscle. Cook until the thermometer registers an internal temperature of 170° F. 25 to 30 minutes per pound should be allowed for roasting time. Before the ham is done, take from the oven and remove the rind. Mark fat into squares. Place whole clove in each square. Pour a honey glaze over ham. Return to oven to finish baking. Baste frequently.

Honey Glazes

• Chopped maraschino cherries and whole almonds mixed with 1 cup honey.
  1 cup honey mixed with 1 cup apricot pulp. (For attractiveness use apricot halves in flower design with whole cloves or angelica as stems.)
  Crushed pineapple with 1 cup honey.
  Tart cherries and honey.
  1 cup honey—½ cup orange juice.
  1 cup honey—½ cup cranberry sauce.
  1 cup honey—½ cup cider.

  For decoration use orange slices and maraschino cherries held in place on ham with cloves.

Raisin Sauce

1 cup quartered or seedless raisins
1 cup water
¼ cup honey
1 tablespoon lemon juice

• Put raisins and water in sauce pan. Simmer until raisins are softened. Add honey. Boil gently for fifteen minutes. Just before serving add lemon juice.

44

Sweet Horseradish Sauce

¼ cup honey
¼ cup mayonnaise
½ cup whipping cream
3 tablespoons horseradish
1 teaspoon mustard
¼ teaspoon salt
1 teaspoon vinegar

•Add honey to mayonnaise. Fold in the whipped cream. Add horseradish, mustard, salt, and vinegar. Store in refrigerator until ready to use.

Honey Spiced Broiled Ham

1 slice ham, 1-inch thick
¾ cup honey
½ teaspoon cloves
½ teaspoon allspice
½ teaspoon cinnamon

• Wipe meat with a damp cloth. Place meat on a broiler rack allowing three inches between the top of the meat and source of heat, if possible. Sprinkle with spices and cook until browned, basting with the honey occasionally. When brown, turn. Sprinkle other side with remaining spices and continue cooking, basting occasionally with remaining honey.

Canadian Bacon, Fruited and Honeyed

6 slices Canadian Style Bacon
1 cup water
1 cup honey
1 cup raisins
6 slices pineapple

• Have bacon sliced one-half inch thick. Place in dripping pan and into an oven of 350° F. Bring water to the boiling point, add the honey, stir until well mixed; then add the raisins and simmer for 10 minutes. When the meat has been in the oven 1 hour, place a slice of pineapple over each piece of bacon, pour the honey sirup containing the raisins over the bacon and pineapple. Return to the oven for 15 minutes.

Lamb Chops with Honey-Mint Sauce

• Select rib, loin or shoulder lamb chops. Set the regulator of the range for broiling. Place the chops so that there is a distance of about three inches between the top of the chops and the source of heat. If the distance must be less, reduce the temperature accordingly so that the chops will broil at a moderate temperature. When the chops are browned on one side, season, turn and finish the cooking on the second side. Frequently during broiling, baste with honey-mint sauce. Chops cut 1-inch thick require 12 to 15 minutes for broiling.

Honey-Mint Sauce

½ cup water
1 tablespoon vinegar
1 cup honey
¼ cup chopped mint

• Heat the water and the vinegar. Add the honey, stir well, then add the chopped mint. Cook slowly for five minutes. This sauce can be used to baste lamb chops or lamb roast during cooking or can be served with the meat at the table.

45

S A L A D S

"If honey is used with the fruit
The flavor will your palate suit."

Fruit Salad

white grapes
1 orange
1 banana
1 pear or peach
1 small apple
1 lemon
lettuce

• Cut grapes into halves and remove seeds. Cut orange into halves and remove sections with a sharp-pointed knife. Slice banana and pear, or peach, and dice the apple. Pour juice of lemon over apple and banana. Moisten all fruit with honey and serve on crisp lettuce or chicory.

Pear Salad

Pears
Pimento cheese
Honey French Dressing
Lettuce

• If canned pears are used, place can in refrigerator to chill pears before making up salad. Allow ½ pear to a person. Place cut side down on lettuce. Cover pear with riced pimento cheese and serve with Honey French Dressing. Rice cheese the same way one rices potatoes.

French Salad Bowl

• Place a crust of bread rubbed with garlic in large bowl while tossing the salad with Honey French Dressing. Use any one or a combination of crisp salad greens such as lettuce, romaine, watercress, endive, pepper grass, or chicory. Serve at once.

Avocado Pear Salad

• Combine equal parts of honey and lemon juice. Beat well and serve over slices of avocado pear and sections of grapefruit on crisp lettuce. Garnish with berries. Suggestion: A dash of paprika or chopped parsley may be added if desired.

46

Fruit Salad Platter

• Place a small dish filled with salad dressing in center of a large platter. Place a large cup-like lettuce leaf for each person around the bowl. In each lettuce leaf place canned pear half, fig, peach, cherries, or other fruit. Prunes stuffed with equal parts peanut butter and honey, or cream cheese and honey, may be placed between salads for garnish, or a cheese ball made by adding enough honey to cream cheese to soften. Make into ball shape and roll in finely chopped nut meats or finely chopped parsley.

Stuffed Tomato Salad

• Select even-sized, firm red tomatoes. Wash, scald in boiling water to loosen skin. Remove skin. Hollow the tomatoes. Sprinkle inside with salt. Drain. Chill. Fill and pile high with (1) chicken or fish salad, (2) cole slaw, (3) cottage cheese and chives. Top with a spoonful of Honey Mayonnaise and stuffed olive.

Fruit Salad Dressing

½ cup lemon juice or other fruit juice
2 teaspoons flour
⅛ teaspoon salt
¼ cup honey
2 eggs yolks
1 cup whipped cream

• Blend lemon juice, flour, salt, and honey until smooth. Cook in the top of double boiler until thickened. Beat yolks of eggs and gradually add the lemon mixture. When well blended return to double boiler and cook about 2 minutes until custard-like in texture. Remove from fire and chill. When ready to use, combine with 1 cup of whipped cream.

Lemon Cream Salad Dressing

3 tablespoons honey
1 tablespoon lemon juice
1 cup whipped cream

• Combine honey and lemon juice. Add to whipped cream. Serve on fruit salad.

French Dressing

½ cup salad oil
½ cup lemon juice
½ cup honey
½ teaspoon paprika
½ teaspoon salt

• Place all in a tightly covered quart jar and shake vigorously just before using.

Roquefort Cheese Dressing

• Crumble with a fork ¼ pound of Roquefort cheese into small pieces. Add to 1 cup of French Dressing.

Thousand Island Dressing

• To one cup Mayonnaise Dressing add finely minced stuffed olives, small onion, a little green pepper, and ½ cup chili sauce. Fold in ½ cup whipped cream.

Frozen Fruit Salad

4   ounces cream cheese
3   tablespoons mayonnaise
2   tablespoons honey
1   cup pitted white cherries
3   slices of pineapple
½   pint whipping cream

• Mix cream cheese with mayonnaise, add honey and mix well. Add cherries and pineapple and fold in whipped cream. Place in freezing tray.

Honey French Dressing

½   cup honey
1   cup salad oil
½   teaspoon salt
⅛   cup chili sauce
½   cup vinegar
1   medium onion grated
1   tablespoon Worcestershire sauce

• Place all ingredients in a quart jar and shake well. Serve this dressing on the lettuce and place a portion of the frozen salad on top. This dressing may be used on other salads.

Boiled Dressing

1   teaspoon mustard
1   teaspoon salt
⅛   teaspoon cayenne
2   tablespoons flour
1   cup milk
3   tablespoons honey
2   egg yolks
½   cup vinegar
1   tablespoon butter

• Mix dry ingredients in top of double boiler, add milk, honey, and egg yolks. Stir well. Cook over hot water until thickened. Add vinegar and butter. Mix well until smooth mixture is formed.

Salad Dressing for Fruit

1 egg
1 tablespoon cornstarch
   pinch salt
2 tablespoons honey
1 cup pineapple juice
2 tablespoons lemon juice

• Put slightly beaten egg, cornstarch, salt, and honey in top of double boiler. Add juices. Cook slowly over hot water until mixture thickens.

Cole Slaw

4 cups finely shredded cabbage

• Beat 1 cup sour cream (cold) until thick. Add ¼ cup vinegar, ¼ cup honey, 1 teaspoon salt, and 2 teaspoons celery salt.

SANDWICHES

"Let honey add that flavor rare
To sandwiches that you prepare."

Honey Butter

½ cup butter
½ to 1 cup honey

● Cream butter well. Add honey gradually. Beat thoroughly. Place in refrigerator. Delicious on toast, hot breads, waffles, and for sandwich filling.

Rolled Sandwich

● Spread creamed honey butter on cut end of bread loaf. Cut slice of bread thin and remove crust. Sprinkle chopped nuts on honey butter. Roll slice and fasten with toothpick. Seal open edge with honey butter. Cover with waxed paper. Place in refrigerator to chill.

Tea Sandwich

● With a biscuit cutter cut circles from bread slices. Spread circles of bread with softened butter and top with cream cheese softened with honey. On this spread red raspberry jam. Place a dot of cream cheese mixture or whipped cream in the center.

Toasted Tea Sandwich

● Use circles cut from bread as in above recipe. Toast until brown on both sides. Spread with honey butter. Sprinkle with chopped nuts. Place under broiler until nuts are slightly browned and serve while hot.

Cream Cheese Sandwich Filling

● Soften cream cheese with enough honey to spread well. Add chopped raisins or nuts.

Fruit Filling

¼ cup each dried p r u n e s, dates, figs, orange peel
1 tablespoon candied ginger
¼ cup honey

● Chop fruit and blend with honey. Use between slices of buttered bread.

49

V E G E T A B L E S

"Here honey lends refining touch
If not too spare or not too much."

Baked Squash

• Wash squash and cut in half lengthwise. Remove seeds. To each half add 1 tablespoon of honey and one or two little pork sausage links. Bake at 400° F. until squash is tender and sausages brown.

Glazed Onions or Carrots

• Cook small white onions or carrots in boiling salted water about 20 to 30 minutes, or until tender. Drain. Let stand a few minutes to dry. Melt four tablespoons butter in pan. Add ¼ cup honey. When well blended, add onions or carrots and cook slowly until browned and well glazed. Turn vegetables occasionally for an even glaze.

Candied Sweet Potatoes

• Boil 6 medium-sized sweet potatoes without paring them. When tender drain and remove the skins. Cut in half lengthwise and arrange in a buttered baking dish. Season with salt. Heat ¼ cup butter, ½ cup honey, ½ cup orange juice, add to potatoes. Bake in quick oven (400° F.) until potatoes are brown.

Sweet-Sour Cabbage

4   cups shredded cabbage
½ cup diced bacon
3   tablespoons flour
¼ cup honey
¼ cup vinegar
½ cup water
1   teaspoon onion, chopped

• Cook shredded cabbage in boiling salted water until tender. Drain. Dice bacon. Cook until well done. Remove bacon and place on cabbage. Blend bacon fat with flour. Add honey, vinegar, water, and chopped onion. Cook until thickened. Pour over cabbage and bacon. Season to taste. Heat thoroughly. Serve hot.

Note: This same recipe may be used with cooked potatoes instead of cabbage.

50

Sweet Potato Orange Casserole

6   cooked and sliced sweet potatoes
1/4   cup butter
2   small oranges
1/2   cup honey
1/2   cup orange juice
1/4   cup bread crumbs

• Place a layer of sliced sweet potatoes in a greased baking dish. Dot with butter and place a layer of sliced orange (not peeled) on top. Repeat this arrangement of sweet potatoes and orange slices. Mix honey with orange juice and pour over all. Cover with buttered bread crumbs. Cover and bake about 30 minutes at 375° F. Remove cover last 10 minutes to brown crumbs.

Family Beets

Slice cooked beets. Keep warm. Cover with the following sauce:

1   tablespoon cornstarch
1/2   cup vinegar
  a few whole cloves
3/4   cup honey
1   tablespoon butter

• Add cornstarch, vinegar, and a few whole cloves (mixed together) to honey. Bring to a slow boil and boil 5 minutes. Add butter. Pour over beets and let stand 20 minutes. Serve hot.

Scalloped Tomatoes

2   cups cooked tomatoes
1/2   teaspoon salt
  pepper
2   tablespoons butter
2   tablespoons honey
1   cup cracker crumbs

• Cover bottom of buttered baking dish with a layer of tomatoes. On this sprinkle salt, pepper, dots of butter and honey. Cover with a layer of cracker crumbs. Repeat with another layer of tomatoes, crumbs, and seasoning. Bake 20 minutes in a hot oven.

Baked Beans

• Soak 2 cups washed beans in 4 cups of cold water over night. In the morning drain off any water that has not been absorbed. Cover the beans with fresh cold water and cook over a low flame in a tightly-covered saucepan. Do not allow the beans to boil. Let them simmer for 1 1/4 hours. Again drain the beans, saving the water. Prepare the bean pot by placing about 1/2 pound of scored salt pork in the bottom. Add the beans, cover with the following mixture: use the bean water that has been drained from the beans, and add to it 1/2 cup of honey; if no bean water was left over, use plain boiling water. Mix 1 teaspoon salt, 1 teaspoon dry mustard, 1 teaspoon ginger, if desired, and 1 tablespoon of finely-chopped onion with a little of the honey water. Add remainder of the honey bean water to this seasoning and pour over the beans. Place small pieces of salt pork on top. (Bacon may be used.) Cover bean pot and bake in a slow oven about 6 hours. Uncover the bean pot during the last hour of baking. If the beans become too dry, it may be necessary to add a little water.

HONEY RECIPES BOOK

BREADS AND PASTRIES

Honey Applesauce Oatmeal Bread

½ cup honey
½ cup shortening
1 cup canned applesauce
⅜ cup lukewarm milk
1 tablespoon honey
2 packages active dry yeast
2 eggs
3 cups sifted all-purpose flour
1 cup rolled oats
1½ teaspoons salt
applesauce topping
Cinnamon
Nutmeg

Combine honey, shortening and applesauce. Heat until shortening melts. Cool to lukewarm. Combine milk, 1 tablespoon honey and yeast, stirring until yeast dissolves. Let stand 5 to 10 minutes. Beat eggs in large bowl. Add lukewarm applesauce mixture, yeast mixture and flour. Mix to smooth batter. Add oats and salt; mix well. Cover and let rise until double in bulk. Beat batter again, spread batter in a greased 8″ round spring form pan. Spread Topping on dough. (See below for recipe.) Sprinkle with nuts, cinnamon and nutmeg. Cover and let rise until double in bulk. Bake in 375° F. oven, 50 to 60 minutes or until done.

Applesauce Topping

1 cup canned applesauce.
2 tablespoons butter
¼ cup honey
½ cup flaked coconut

Slowly cook applesauce down to ½ cup; combine with remaining ingredients.

Brown Nut Bread With Honey Glaze

3 cups whole-wheat flour
2 cups buttermilk
½ cup honey
2 tablespoons sugar
3 teaspoons soda
1 teaspoon salt
¼ teaspoon nutmeg
1 cup chopped pecan meats, or nuts desired

Mix dry ingredients well. Blend honey with milk and mix into dry ingredients. Grease one 9″ x 5″ x 3″ loaf pan and pour in mixture. Bake in 350° F. oven for 45 minutes or until done. Just before taking out, glaze top with 1 tablespoon honey mixed with 1 tablespoon melted butter. Sprinkle over chopped pecans. Return to oven and let glaze for 5 minutes.

Quick Honey Orange Rolls

1 tablespoon orange juice
2 teaspoons grated orange rind
½ cup strained honey
¼ cup butter
2 cups prepared biscuit mix (or 1 biscuit recipe using 2 cups flour)
¾ cup milk

Make a thin syrup with the orange juice, grated rind, honey and butter. Pour equal amounts of it into 8 greased custard cups. Blend the biscuit mix with the milk, and drop an equal amount of the dough into each cup. Bake in a hot oven, 450° F., 12 to 15 minutes.

Apple-Orange Honey Loaf

2 large oranges
1 cup seedless raisins
2 cups canned applesauce
1 cup honey
4 cups sifted all-purpose flour
4 teaspoons baking powder
1½ teaspoons baking soda
1 cup sugar
1½ teaspoons salt
1½ cups chopped nuts
2 eggs, beaten
6 tablespoons melted butter or margarine

Squeeze juice from oranges. Using medium blade, put rind and raisins through food chopper. Add orange juice, rind and raisins to applesauce; stir in honey. Sift together flour, baking powder, baking soda, sugar and salt; add applesauce mixture and nuts. Mix thoroughly. Add eggs and melted butter or margarine; stir until thoroughly blended. Pour into 2 greased loaf pans 9″ x 5″ x 3″. Bake in moderate oven, 350° F., 1 hour and 15 minutes. Remove from pans and cool on wire rack. The bread will slice better if allowed to stand 12 hours.

Honey-Filled Coffee Cake

2 packages granular or compressed yeast
¼ cup lukewarm water
½ cup shortening
2 teaspoons salt
¼ cup sugar
1 cup scalded milk
2 eggs, beaten
4½ cups sifted flour
Honey Filling

Sprinkle granular yeast over warm (110° F.) water; or crumble compressed yeast over lukewarm (85° F.) water. Let stand until thoroughly dissolved (5 to 15 minutes).

Combine shortening, salt and sugar in large bowl; add scalded milk. Stir until shortening is melted, then cool until lukewarm.

Add eggs and yeast; mix well.

Add flour gradually, beating thoroughly after each addition. Turn onto lightly floured board and knead to a smooth dough.

Place in greased bowl and brush top of dough with melted shortening. Cover; let rise in warm place until light and doubled (about 1½ hours).

Punch down and let rest 10 minutes. Turn out onto floured board. Divide dough in two, keeping one half covered with cloth.

Roll out the other half into a rectangle, about 12″ x 16″. Brush with melted butter and spread with half the Honey Filling. (See below for recipe.) Roll like jelly roll; seal edges.

Cut into 1″ slices; make bottom layer in 10″ greased tube pan, placing slices (cut side down) so they barely touch. Arrange remaining slices in layers, covering up the spaces—with no slice directly on top of another. (This gives an interesting swirl pattern when coffee cake is sliced.)

Prepare remaining half of dough in same manner, placing slices on top in layers as before. Cover and let rise in warm place about 30 minutes or until doubled.

Bake in moderate oven (350° F.) 45 to 60 minutes, or until sides and top are well browned. (If bread browns too soon, cover with foil the last half of baking.)

Loosen bread from pan; turn out on rack to cool. If desired, pour over glaze made by simmering together until thick (about 5 minutes): ½ c. honey, ½ c. sugar, 1 tblsp. butter or margarine and 1 tblsp. coarsely grated orange rind. Pour glaze over bread.

Honey Filling: Combine ½ c. honey, ¼ c. sugar, grated rind of 1 orange or lemon, 1 tblsp. orange or lemon juice, 1 tsp. cinnamon, ⅓ c. raisins, cut fine, ⅓ c. nuts, chopped fine and 1 tblsp. melted butter or margarine.

Honey Pecan Wheat Rolls

1 cup milk
3 tablespoons molasses
2 tablespoons honey
2½ teaspoons salt
4 tablespoons shortening
½ cup warm, not hot, water (lukewarm for compressed yeast)
1 package or cake yeast active, dry
   or compressed
2¼ cups whole-wheat flour
2¼ cups enriched flour

Honey Syrup
⅓ cup brown sugar
⅔ cup honey
3 tablespoons butter
Stir and combine

Scald milk. Stir in molasses, honey, salt and shortening; cool to lukewarm. Measure water into a large mixing bowl. Sprinkle or crumble in yeast. Stir until dissolved. Stir in lukewarm milk mixture. Mix flours; add about half to the liquid. Beat until smooth. Add remaining flour. Turn out on lightly floured board. Knead until smooth and elastic. Place in a greased bowl. Brush top with shortening. Cover; let rise in a warm place, free from draft, about 1 hour and 20 minutes, until doubled in bulk. Punch down. Turn out on lightly floured board.

Spread ½ the Honey Syrup in each of 2 pans 8″ x 8″ x 2″. Arrange half the pecans in each pan. Divide dough in half. Form each half into a 12 inch roll. Cut into 12 equal pieces. Form into balls.

Place in prepared pans about ¼" apart. Cover; let rise in a warm place, free from draft, about 1 hour, until doubled in bulk.

Bake at 400° F. about 25 minutes. Turn out of pans immediately. Makes 2 dozen.

Basic Sweet Dough For Honey Rose Buds

½ cup milk
½ cup sugar
¼ cup shortening
1½ teaspoons salt
½ cup warm, not hot, water
2 packages or cakes of yeast, active dry or compressed
2 eggs, beaten
5 cups sifted enriched flour

Scald milk; stir in sugar, shortening and salt. Cool to lukewarm. Measure water into a large mixing bowl (warm, not hot, for active dry yeast, lukewarm for compressed yeast). Sprinkle or crumble in yeast; stir until dissolved. Blend in lukewarm milk mixture. Add egg and about half the flour. Beat until smooth. Stir in remaining flour to form a soft dough. Turn out on a floured board. Knead until smooth and elastic. Place in greased bowl. Brush with softened shortening. Cover; let rise in warm place, free from draft, about 1 hour until doubled in bulk. Punch down. Note: Dough may be used with many toppings. See below for one recipe.

Honey Rose Bud Topping

¼ cup honey
⅓ cup chopped nuts
½ cup dried currants or chopped raisins

Divide Sweet Dough in half. Roll each half into a square about 12 inches by 12 inches. Brush each square with honey. Sprinkle with currants and chopped nuts. Roll as for jelly roll. Cut into 12 equal pieces. Place cut side up in greased muffin pans. With sharp knife or scissors, cut crosses about ½ inch deep across top of buns.

Cover. Let rise in a warm place, free from draft, until doubled in bulk.

Bake at 350° F. about 30 minutes.

Quick Applesauce Pinwheels

2 cups canned applesauce
2 tablespoons butter or margarine
⅓ cup honey
⅔ cup seedless raisins
1 package roll mix
2 tablespoons sugar
Cinnamon

Combine applesauce, butter or margarine and honey; cook 15 to 20 minutes to evaporate some of the moisture and thicken. Add raisins; cool. Prepare roll mix according to directions on package, adding sugar to roll mix. After dough has risen double in bulk, knead. Roll out in oblong 15" x 11" x ½"; spread with applesauce mixture. Sprinkle generously with cinnamon. Roll up like jelly roll. Cut in 1" slices. Place slices close together in greased 9" x 9" x 2" pan, cut side up. Cover; let rise until double in bulk. Bake in hot oven, 400° F., for 25 minutes. Serve hot.

Honey Buns

¼ cup warm water
1 teaspoon sugar
1 package granular or compressed yeast
½ cup shortening
½ cup sugar
1 teaspoon salt
3 cups sifted flour
¾ cup water
1 egg, well beaten
½ cup honey
½ cup chopped nuts

Combine warm water and 1 tsp. sugar. Sprinkle granular yeast over warm (110° F.) mixture; or crumble compressed yeast over lukewarm (85° F.) mixture. Let stand 5 minutes.

Cream shortening, ½ c. sugar and salt. Mix in 1 c. flour and ¾ c. water. Add to yeast mixture.

Stir in 2 cups flour, and egg; cover and refrigerate overnight.

Grease muffin pans, enough for 24 buns. In each muffin cup put 1 tsp. each honey and nuts. Drop 1 tblsp. of dough in each muffin cup. Let rise in warm place until doubled.

Bake in 375° F. oven 12 to 15 minutes. Serve upside down.

Honey Bun Coffee Cake

1   package yeast, compressed or dry
¼ cup water (lukewarm for compressed
     yeast, warm for dry)
½ cup milk
¼ cup sugar
1   teaspoon salt
2   tablespoons shortening
1   egg
1   teaspoon grated lemon rind
     (if desired)
3   cups sifted enriched flour
¼ cup butter or margarine
2   tablespoons honey
1   egg white
1   cup confectioners' sugar

Soften yeast in water. Scald milk. Measure sugar, salt and shortening into medium size mixing bowl. Cool to lukewarm. Add flour (about 1 cup) to make a thick batter. Mix well. Add softened yeast, egg and lemon rind. Beat well. Add enough more flour (about 1½ cups) to make a soft dough. Turn out on lightly floured board or pastry cloth and knead until smooth and satiny. Place in greased bowl. Cover and let rise until doubled (about 1½ hours). When light, punch down and let rest 10 minutes. Divide dough into 12 equal pieces. Roll each piece under palm of hands to roll about 8″ long and ¾″ in diameter. Make 6 of the rolls into "U" shaped pieces and arrange side by side in bottom of greased 9″ round pan with ends toward center forming a scalloped circle. Make remaining 6 rolls into oval shaped pieces. Arrange pieces in pan so that ends meet in the center and each oval covers joining ends of two "U" shaped pieces. Cream together butter or margarine and honey. Add unbeaten egg white. Mix well. Add sugar and blend thoroughly. Pour over coffee cake in pan. Let rise until doubled (about 45 minutes). Bake in moderate oven (350° F.) about 25 minutes.

Possibly the earliest proof of man's use of honey is a prehistoric painting found in Valencia, Spain, and estimated to be about 15,000 years old. The painting shows a woman gathering honey from a hole in a cliff.

Honey Whole-Wheat Muffins

1   cup sifted all-purpose flour
2   teaspoons baking powder
½ teaspoon salt
½ cup unsifted whole-wheat flour
½ cup milk
1   egg, well beaten
½ cup honey
½ cup coarsely-chopped cooked
     prunes
1   teaspoon grated orange peel
¼ cup salad oil or melted shortening

Preheat oven to 400° F. Grease bottoms of 12 (2½″) muffin-pan cups, or line each with paper.

Sift all-purpose flour with baking powder and salt into large bowl. Stir in whole-wheat flour; mix well.

Combine milk and rest of ingredients in medium bowl; beat well with wooden spoon.

Make a well in center of dry ingredients. Pour in milk mixture all at once; stir quickly, with fork, just until dry ingredients are moistened. Do not beat. Batter will be lumpy.

Quickly dip batter into muffin-pan cups, filling not quite two-thirds full. Bake 20 to 25 minutes, or until nicely browned.

Loosen edge of each muffin with spatula; turn out. Serve hot.

Honey Marmalade Nut Bread

2½ cups sifted all-purpose flour
1   tablespoon baking powder
1   teaspoon salt
½ cup honey
2   tablespoons soft butter or
     margarine
3   eggs, beaten
1   cup orange marmalade
1   tablespoon grated orange peel
1   cup finely chopped walnuts or
     pecans

Sift flour with baking powder and salt;
set aside.

In medium bowl, with wooden spoon,
beat honey, butter, and eggs until smooth.

Stir in marmalade and orange peel, mixing well. Add flour mixture, stirring until well combined. Stir in nuts.

Turn into prepared pan; bake in 350° F.
oven about 1 hour, or until cake tester
inserted in center comes out clean.

Let cool in pan 10 minutes. Remove
from pan; cool completely on wire rack.
Cut into thin slices and serve with butter
or cream cheese.

Walnut Honey Loaf

1   cup honey
1   cup milk
½ cup sugar
2½ cups sifted flour
1   teaspoon soda
1   teaspoon salt
½ cup walnuts (chopped)
¼ cup shortening
2   egg yolks (or 1 egg)

Combine honey, milk, and sugar in a 3-
quart saucepan. Heat over medium heat,
stirring constantly, just until sugar is
dissolved. (Mixture will be lukewarm).
Cool. Sift together the sifted flour, soda,
salt. Add to honey mixture together with
walnuts, shortening and egg yolks. Beat
for 2 minutes (300 strokes) until well
blended. Turn into well-greased and
floured 9″ x 5″ x 3″ pan, or line with
heavy waxed paper and grease. Bake in
325° F. oven 75 to 90 minutes or until done.
Cool for 15 minutes, then remove from pan
and let cool on wire rack. Drizzle over a
thin glaze if desired.

Quick Honey Coconut Buns

3   cups sifted flour
3¾ teaspoons double-acting baking
     powder
1   teaspoon salt
⅓ cup granulated sugar
½ cup shortening
1   cup milk
1   egg, beaten
⅓ cup firmly-packed brown sugar
1½ teaspoons ground cinnamon
½ teaspoon salt
¾ teaspoon orange rind
2½ tablespoons butter
⅓ cup honey
¾ cup flaked coconut

Sift flour once, measure, add baking
powder, salt, and sugar, and sift again.
Cut in shortening. Combine milk and egg

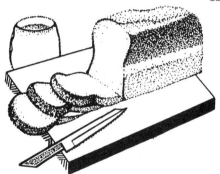

and add to flour mixture. Stir with fork
until soft dough is formed (about 20
strokes). Turn out on lightly-floured board
and knead 30 seconds. Roll into a 15″ x 10″
rectangle, ¼″ thick.
Mix together brown sugar, cinnamon,
salt, orange rind, butter, and honey.
Spread half of the mixture on dough and
sprinkle with half of the coconut. Roll
as for jelly roll and cut in 1″ slices.
Arrange cut side down in lightly-greased
muffin tins. Spread top with remaining
brown sugar mixture and sprinkle with
remaining coconut. Bake in hot oven (425°
F.) 20 minutes, or until done.

*It takes 556 worker bees flying the equi-
valent of 1 1/3 times around the world to
produce just one pound of honey.*

CAKES AND ICINGS

Super Delicious Chocolate Cake

3   squares unsweetened chocolate, melted
⅔ cup honey
1¾ cups sifted cake flour
1   teaspoon soda
¾ teaspoon salt
½ cup butter or other shortening
½ cup sugar
1   teaspoon vanilla extract
2   eggs, unbeaten
⅔ cup water

Blend chocolate and honey; cool to lukewarm. Sift flour once, measure, add soda and salt, and sift together three times. Cream butter thoroughly, add sugar gradually, and cream together until light and fluffy. Add chocolate-honey mixture and vanilla. Blend. Add eggs, one at a time, beating thoroughly after each addition. Add flour, alternately with water, a small amount at a time, beating after each addition until smooth. Bake in two greased and floured 8" layer pans in 350° F. oven 30 to 35 minutes. Spread with French Honey Chocolate Frosting.

French Honey Chocolate Frosting

½ cup sugar
¼ cup butter
¼ cup light cream
¼ cup honey
¼ teaspoon salt
3   squares unsweetened chocolate, cut into small pieces
2   egg yolks, well beaten

Combine sugar, butter, cream, honey, salt, and chocolate in top of double boiler. Place over boiling water. When chocolate is melted, beat with rotary beater until blended. Pour small amount of mixture over egg yolks, stirring vigorously. Return to double boiler and cook 2 minutes longer, or until mixture thickens slightly, stirring constantly. Remove from hot water, place in pan of ice water or cracked ice, and beat until of right consistency to spread.

The honey bee is one of the oldest forms of life on earth today. It has hardly changed form or life style except to adapt to changing climate and surroundings.

Elegant White Fruit Cake

1   cup cooking oil
1½ cups honey
4   eggs
3   cups sifted flour
1   teaspoon baking powder
¾ teaspoon baking soda
2   teaspoons salt
¾ cup apple juice or pineapple juice
1   pound candied cherries
1   pound candied pineapple
1   pound dates, pitted and cut up
7 to 8 cups pecans

Preheat oven to 275° F. Mix together cooking oil, honey and eggs in mixing bowl. Beat 2 minutes. Sift together 2 cups flour (sifted before measuring), baking powder, soda and salt. Stir in oil-honey mixture alternately with ¾ cup juice.

Combine candied fruit and dust thoroughly with remaining cup of flour. Then pour batter over fruit, mixing well. Line 2 greased loaf pans or a greased tube spring form pan with brown paper. Fill with cake batter. Bake at 275° F. for 2½ to 3 hours. Cool before removing from pan. Wrap in foil and store in covered container.

Honey Orange Cake

2   cups sifted cake flour
3½ teaspoons baking powder
¾ teaspoon salt
½ cup butter or other shortening
½ cup sugar
⅔ cup honey
2   egg yolks
½ cup orange juice
2   egg whites, stiffly beaten

Sift flour once, measure, add baking powder and salt, and sift together three times. Cream butter thoroughly, add sugar gradually, and cream together until light and fluffy. Add honey. Blend. Add egg yolks and beat thoroughly. Add flour, alternately with orange juice, a small amount at a time, beating after each addition until smooth. Fold in egg whites. Bake in two greased 9" layer pans in 350° F. oven 30 to 35 minutes.

Delicious Valentine Cake

3 squares unsweetened chocolate, melted
⅔ cup honey
1¾ cups sifted cake flour
1 teaspoon soda
¾ teaspoon salt
½ cup butter or other shortening
½ cup sugar
1 teaspoon vanilla extract
2 eggs, unbeaten
⅔ cup water

Blend chocolate and honey; cool to lukewarm. Sift flour once, measure, add soda and salt, and sift together three times. Cream butter thoroughly, add sugar gradually, and cream together until light and fluffy. Add chocolate-honey mixture and vanilla. Blend. Add eggs, one at a time, beating thoroughly after each addition. Add flour, alternately with water, a small amount at a time, beating after each addition until smooth. Bake in two greased 8" layer pans or heart shaped pans at 350° F. for 30 to 35 minutes. Spread with Fluffy Honey Meringue. Sprinkle sides of cake with flaked coconut and decorate with candy hearts.

Fluffy Honey Meringue

2 egg whites
Dash of salt
1 cup honey

Beat egg whites with salt until stiff enough to hold up in peaks, but not dry. Pour honey in fine stream over egg whites, beating constantly about 10 to 15 minutes, or until frosting holds its shape or beat about 2½ minutes at high speed of electric mixer. This meringue makes a delicious topping for any cake or pudding.

Spice Cake and Bananas with Honey Custard Sauce

1 package of spice cake mix
2 ripe bananas
Honey Custard Sauce

Prepare cake mix according to package directions and bake in 8" x 12" baking pan. Cake may be served slightly warm or cold with sliced bananas on top and Honey Custard Sauce poured over.

Honey Custard Sauce

2 eggs
⅓ cup honey
⅛ teaspoon salt
1⅔ cups evaporated milk (1 tall can)
1 cup boiling water
½ teaspoon vanilla extract
⅛ teaspoon nutmeg

Beat eggs in top of double boiler. Add honey and salt. Blend well, then add milk. Stir in the boiling water. Cook over boiling water, stirring constantly until mixture just coats a spoon, about 4 to 5 minutes. Remove from heat immediately and place top of double boiler in cold water to hasten cooling and keep mixture from further cooking. Stir frequently while cooling. Add vanilla and nutmeg. Makes about 3 cups sauce.

Honey Lemon Layer Cake

½ cup shortening
1 cup honey
2 eggs
2 cups sifted cake flour
¾ teaspoon baking soda
½ teaspoon salt
¼ cup milk
2 tablespoons lemon juice

Cream together shortening and honey.

Add eggs, one at a time, beating well after each addition.

Sift together flour, baking soda and salt.

Sour milk with lemon juice. Add sifted dry ingredients alternately with sour milk to egg mixture.

Pour into 2 greased 8" layer cake pans. Bake in moderate oven (350° F.) 25 to 30 minutes. Frost with Honey Cream Cheese Frosting and decorate with lemon candy slices or peach slices and cherries.

Honey Cream Cheese Frosting

1 3 oz. package cream cheese
1 tablespoon honey
2½ cups sifted confectioners' sugar
½ pound lemon fruit candy slices or peach slices and cherries

Blend cheese with honey. Gradually add sugar; beat until smooth.

All-Honey Chocolate Cake

2   cups sifted cake flour
1½ teaspoons soda
½   teaspoon salt
½   cup shortening
1¼ cups honey
2   eggs
3   squares unsweetened chocolate,
       melted
⅔   cup water
1   teaspoon vanilla

Sift flour once, measure, add soda and salt, and sift together three times. Cream shortening; gradually add honey, beating well after each addition to keep mixture thick. Add ¼ of flour mixture and beat until smooth and well blended. Add eggs, one at a time, beating well after each. Stir in chocolate and blend. Add remaining flour alternately with water, beating very well after each addition. Add vanilla. Bake in two greased, 9″ layer pans at 350° F. for 30 minutes, or until done. Frost and fill with Quick Creamed Frosting.

Quick Creamed Frosting

½   cup honey
½   cup butter
1   teaspoon vanilla
2   egg whites
1   cup sifted confectioners' sugar
1   square unsweetened chocolate, melted

Cream honey and butter. Stir in vanilla. Beat egg whites until they form soft peaks. Add sifted confectioners' sugar gradually, beating after each addition. Fold egg white mixture gradually into honey mixture. Add melted chocolate to ⅓ of frosting. Use the chocolate part between the layers. Spread the white frosting on top and sides of cake.

Honey Upside-Down Cake with Honey Sauce

½   cup honey
¼   cup butter
4 or 5 unpeeled apples
       Pecan halves
       Maraschino cherries

Put honey and butter in a heavy, medium-sized iron .skillet and let slowly melt on top of stove. Core the unpeeled apples, and cut them crosswise into ring slices ¾″ thick, preparing enough slices to cover bottom of skillet. Add the apple rings to honey and butter and simmer until apples are partly cooked, turning once. Place a maraschino cherry in center of each apple ring, and nut meat halves (pecans) in the spaces around the apples. Pour the following batter over the hot mixture:

½   cup butter
¾   cup honey
1   egg
½   cup milk
1½ cups flour
1   teaspoon baking powder
¼   teaspoon soda
¼   teaspoon cinnamon
½   teaspoon nutmeg
⅛   teaspoon ginger

Cream together the butter and honey; add egg and beat until smooth. Add milk alternately with sifted dry ingredients. Bake in heavy skillet at 350° F. 30 to 35 minutes. Turn upside-down cake onto a large platter. This may be served hot or cold with sauce made of ½ cup of honey combined with ½ cup butter, heated.

Old-Fashioned Honey Cake

1   cup butter
1   cup sugar
3   eggs
1   teaspoon soda
1   cup honey
3   cups sifted flour
1   teaspoon baking powder
1   teaspoon cinnamon
½ teaspoon ginger
¼ teaspoon nutmeg
¼ teaspoon ground cloves
1   cup milk

Cream butter and sugar, beat in eggs. Add soda to honey. Sift all dry ingredients together. Add alternately honey and milk with dry ingredients to creamed mixture. Blend well. Bake in a 13" x 9" x 2" pan in a 350° F. oven for 45 to 50 minutes. Delicious with a quickie topping of honey drizzled over hot cake and sprinkled with a mixture of sugar and cinnamon.

Honey Bunny Cake

½ cup shortening
¾ cup honey
¾ cup milk
1½ teaspoons vanilla
¼ teaspoon almond extract
2¼ cups sifted cake flour
3¼ teaspoons double-acting baking powder
1   teaspoon salt
¾ cup sugar
4   egg whites, unbeaten

Cream shortening with honey until well blended. To the milk add vanilla and almond extract. Sift dry ingredients and add. Add ½ cup of the milk. Mix until all flour is dampened. Beat well. Add egg whites and remaining milk and beat a minute or two longer. Pour batter into 13" x 9" x 2" pan that has been greased and bottom lined with paper. Bake in moderate oven (350° F.) 25 to 30 minutes, or until done.

To make bunny's head, first cut two strips from one end of cake, each 1½" wide. These strips are for ears. Remaining piece is for face. Set face piece on large platter or tray, using the longer edges of cake for top and bottom of face. Place the two ear strips against top edge of face, slanting them outward slightly. Frost with Fluffy Honey Frosting given with the Delicious Valentine Cake.

Spread frosting over top and sides of face and ears. Sprinkle with about 1⅓ cups flaked coconut. If desired, tint some of the coconut pink and sprinkle this along middle of ears. For eyes, nose, and mouth, use jelly beans, gumdrops, or other candies. Twist a licorice stick and use for bow tie.

Choice Honey Fruit Cake

3   cups sifted all-purpose flour
1   teaspoon salt
1½ teaspoons baking soda
½ teaspoon ground cinnamon
½ teaspoon ground mace
½ teaspoon ground allspice
3   cups seedless raisins
3½ cups currants
½ pound or 1¼ cups red & green glace cherries, sliced
1   cup chopped walnuts or pecans
½ cup heavy fruit syrup or sweetened juice
6   tablespoons white vinegar
1   cup shortening
1   cup honey
¼ cup firmly-packed brown sugar
6   eggs, beaten

Sift together 2½ cups flour, salt, baking soda, and spices. Steam raisins and currants over boiling water, spread on paper toweling, and let dry until quite cool. Combine raisins, currants, cherries, and nuts with remaining ½ cup of flour. Combine fruit syrup or sweetened juice and vinegar. Cream together the shortening, honey, and brown sugar; beat until light and creamy. Beat in eggs. Add dry ingredients and liquids alternately, a little of each at a time, stirring in after each addition just enough to blend well. Stir in fruits and nuts. Pour into a 10" tube pan which has been greased, then lined with heavy brown paper also greased. Bake in 300° F. oven for 3 hours. If you prefer, cake may be baked in a long angel food pan 15½" x 4½" x 4½" about 2½ hours.

Meringue Spice Cake

¾ cup shortening
1 cup brown sugar
1 cup honey
2 egg yolks, beaten
2⅓ cups flour
¾ teaspoon salt
2 teaspoons baking powder
1 teaspoon soda
1 teaspoon cinnamon
1 teaspoon cloves
1 cup sour milk
1 teaspoon vanilla

Thoroughly cream shortening, brown sugar and honey; add egg yolks and beat until fluffy. Add sifted dry ingredients alternating with milk and vanilla. Beat vigorously after each addition. Pour into greased 9" x 13" pan. Cover with Brown Sugar Meringue. Bake at 325° F. about 50 minutes.

Brown Sugar Meringue

2 egg whites, stiffly beaten
1 cup brown sugar
½ cup broken nut meats

Slowly add sugar and nuts to egg whites, beat until smooth. Spread over batter and bake as directed.

Honey Cheese Cake

3 tablespoons butter
2 cups sieved cottage cheese
2 tablespoons sifted flour
1 teaspoon salt
⅓ cup honey
3 tablespoons lemon juice
1 teaspoon lemon rind
4 eggs, separated
⅓ cup sugar
⅔ cup milk

Crumb Base

2 cups crushed graham cracker crumbs
½ cup butter, melted
1 teaspoon cinnamon
⅓ cup honey

Cream butter; blend in cottage cheese, flour and salt. Beat in honey, lemon juice and rind.

Add egg yolks, one at a time, beating well after each addition.

Beat egg whites until stiff. Slowly add sugar; beat until soft peaks form. Fold into cheese mixture. Blend in milk.

Combine all ingredients for Crumb Base. Press all but ½ cup mixture firmly along bottom and sides of 11½" x 7½" x 1½" pan.

Pour in filling; sprinkle with remaining crumb mixture. Bake in 350° F. oven 1 hour. Chill for easier cutting.

Chocolate Buttercream Icing

1¾ cups powdered sugar
¾ cup cocoa
¼ teaspoon salt
3 tablespoons butter
3 tablespoons shortening
1 tablespoon honey
1 egg white
2 tablespoons milk

Sift dry ingredients together and place in mixing bowl with remaining ingredients except milk. Mix until smooth.

Add milk and mix at low speed until light.

Chocolate Fudge Icing

1¾ cups powdered sugar
¾ cup cocoa
¼ teaspoon salt
3 tablespoons butter
2 tablespoons shortening
1½ tablespoons honey
1 egg white
2-3 tablespoons hot milk

Have all ingredients at room temperature. Sift dry ingredients together.

Mix in warmed bowl with remainder of ingredients, except milk, until smooth.

Add hot milk and mix until smooth. Keep in warm bowl (115°F.) until used, stirring occasionally. Too high a temperature causes icing to lose its shine.

COOKIES

Honey Raisin Bars

Dough:

1¼ cups sifted flour
3 tablespoons sugar
1 teaspoon baking powder
¼ teaspoon salt
½ cup butter or margarine
1 tablespoon water
1 tablespoon orange peel
1 egg

Filling:

1 tablespoon water
2 teaspoons orange peel
1 egg
½ cup honey
2 tablespoons soft butter or margarine
¾ cup seedless raisins, chopped
¾ cup moist coconut
½ cup pecans, chopped

Honey Glaze:

2 tablespoons honey
1 tablespoon soft butter or margarine
1 tablespoon water
½ teaspoon orange extract
1 cup confectioners' sugar

Sift together the flour, sugar, baking powder and salt. Cut in the butter with a pastry blender until particles are fine. Combine the water, orange peel and the egg. Beat with a rotary beater until light. Add to flour mixture, stirring with fork until dough is moist enough to hold together. Roll out half of the dough on a piece of waxed paper to make a 9" square. Invert into an ungreased 9" square pan; remove paper; pat in place. Press any extra edges up sides of pan. Roll out remainder of dough on waxed paper, same size; set aside.

To make filling, combine water, orange peel and egg. Beat together with a fork. Add honey, butter, chopped raisins, coconut and chopped pecans. Spread over dough in pan. Place remaining dough over filling. Press down lightly; remove paper. Prick top with fork, dip tines in flour. Bake in a 375° F. oven 25 to 35 minutes or until top is lightly browned. Let cool 10 or 15 minutes, then spread with Honey Glaze. To make glaze, combine honey, butter, water, orange extract and confectioners' sugar. Beat until

smooth. Spread over top of cookies. Cool completely before cutting into bars. Makes 2 dozen.

Honey Nut Cookies

2 egg whites
½ cup honey
½ cup sugar
¼ teaspoon salt
¼ cup water
1 tablespoon flavoring
1 cup chopped black walnuts

Beat egg whites with rotary beater until stiff. Gradually add honey, beating after each addition. Continue beating until mixture is stiff. Combine sugar, salt, and water in small saucepan. Cook until sugar is dissolved and mixture boils, stirring constantly. Cover tightly and boil 2 minutes. Uncover and boil, without stirring, until a small amount of syrup forms a firm ball in cold water (250° F.). Pour syrup in fine stream over egg mixture, beating constantly. Beat until cool and thickened. Add flavoring and nuts. Drop from teaspoon on well-buttered floured baking sheet. Bake in slow oven (300° F.) 25 to 30 minutes, or until delicately browned. Carefully remove from sheet with sharp edge of clean knife.

Honey Oatmeal Chews

½ cup butter
½ cup honey
½ cup sugar
1 egg
1 teaspoon vanilla
⅔ cup sifted all-purpose flour
½ teaspoon baking soda
½ teaspoon baking powder
¼ teaspoon salt
1 cup quick-cooking rolled oats
1 cup flaked coconut
½ cup chopped almonds

Cream butter, honey and sugar until light and fluffy. Add egg and vanilla; beat well. Sift together flour, soda, baking powder, and salt. Add to creamed mixture. Stir in oatmeal, coconut, and nuts. Spread in a greased 13½" x 9" baking pan. Bake at 350° F. for 20 to 25 minutes. When cool, cut into bars about 1½" x 2½". Makes 30 bars.

German Honey Cookies

3   ounces each citron, candied orange
     peel and candied lemon peel
1   cup chopped blanched almonds
1   teaspoon grated lemon rind
3   tablespoons ground cinnamon
1   tablespoon ground cloves
3⅓ cups powdered sugar
6   eggs, beaten until light
 ¼ cup orange juice
2   cups honey
2   tablespoons hot water
5   cups sifted all purpose-flour
1   tablespoon soda
     Blanched almonds

Cut citron and candied peels into small pieces and combine. Add chopped almonds, lemon rind, cinnamon, cloves and powdered sugar. Add beaten eggs and orange juice, beating until smooth. Heat honey and the 2 tablespoons hot water until it just reaches the boiling point. Cool until lukewarm. Then stir honey into egg mixture and stir in flour and soda. Cover the dough and let stand in refrigerator or where it is cool for 12 hours or more. Drop by spoonful, well apart, on a greased baking sheet. Bake at 350° F. for 12 to 18 minutes or until light brown. When cool, decorate with blanched almonds or glaze. Makes about 200 2½" cookies.

Lemon or Orange Glaze

1¼ cups confectioners' sugar
 ¼ cup lemon or orange juice

Mix or blend well and spread on warm cookies.

Glazed Christmas Cookies

2   cups sifted all-purpose flour
1   teaspoon baking soda
1   teaspoon salt
 ½ cup soft butter or margarine
1   teaspoon vanilla extract
 ½ teaspoon almond extract
⅔ cup honey
1   egg, well beaten
 ¼ cup vinegar
 ½ cup finely-cut mixed candied peel
 ½ cup finely-cut red or green
     glace cherries
 ½ cup finely-cut shredded coconut
1   egg white, slightly beaten
     Red sugar sand
     Split, blanched almonds

Sift together flour, baking soda, and salt. Cream together butter or margarine, vanilla and almond extracts and honey; beat until fluffy and creamy. Beat in egg and vinegar. Stir in sifted dry ingredients gradually; blend well. Mix in candied peel, cherries, and coconut. Chill dough several hours or overnight. Shape one-quarter of dough at a time, leaving remaining dough in refrigerator. Shape into balls ¾" in diameter. Place 2" apart on greased cooky sheet. Grease the bottom of a 2" diameter glass tumbler, then dip in flour. Press cookies with greased and floured tumbler, dipping tumbler in flour as needed. Brush surface of cookies with slightly-beaten egg white; sprinkle with red sugar. Arrange split blanched almonds in flower-petal pattern on each. Bake in a 375° F. oven about 12 minutes. Remove from pan immediately. Makes about 6 dozen cookies.

Poinsettia Balls

3   cups sifted all-purpose flour
 ½ teaspoon baking soda
 ½ teaspoon salt
1   cup butter or margarine
⅔ cup honey
2   tablespoons grated orange rind
2   eggs, separated
1   tablespoon grated lemon rind
2   tablespoons white vinegar
1½ cups finely-chopped pecans
7   dozen red glace cherries

Sift together flour, baking soda, and

salt. Cream together butter or margarine and honey; beat until light and creamy. Beat in egg yolks until well blended. Beat in orange and lemon rinds and vinegar until well blended. Stir in dry ingredients gradually; mix well. Chill dough for 1 hour. Form into balls about 1" in diameter. Beat egg whites slightly. Dip balls in egg whites, then roll in pecans. Place 2" apart on greased baking sheet. Cut each cherry with scissors from top almost to bottom in thin slices to form petals. "Spread" a cut cherry on top of each ball, spreading petals into a flower. Bake in 325° F. oven for 18 to 20 minutes. Makes 7 dozen cookies.

Fruit Cake Cookies

1   cup sifted all-purpose flour
½ teaspoon baking soda
¼ teaspoon salt
½ teaspoon ground cinnamon
½ teaspoon ground cloves
½ teaspoon ground allspice
⅛ teaspoon ground nutmeg
¼ cup shortening
½ cup honey
¼ cup firmly packed brown sugar
1   egg beaten
2   tablespoons milk
2   tablespoons vinegar
¼ teaspoon imitation rum extract
¼ teaspoon vanilla extract
½ cup seedless raisins
½ cup currants
½ cup finely cut candied pineapple
½ cup finely cut candied citron
¾ cup sliced glace cherries
¾ cup coarsely chopped pecans

Sift together flour, baking soda, salt, and spices. Cream together shortening, honey, and brown sugar; beat until light and creamy. Beat in egg, milk, vinegar, rum and vanilla extracts. Stir in dry ingredients gradually. Mix in fruits and nuts.

Drop from tip of teaspoon onto greased baking sheet. Bake in 325° F. (slow) oven about 20 minutes. Remove from pan immediately. When cooled, frost with confectioners' sugar frosting and garnish with cinnamon red hots, or glace cherries, or colored sugar. Makes 4 dozen cookies.

Honeybee Diamonds

¾ cup butter
¾ cup sugar
3   eggs
1   cup sifted flour
1½ teaspoons baking powder
¼ teaspoon salt
½ teaspoon cinnamon
¼ cup milk
1   teaspoon grated orange peel
1   cup walnuts, chopped

Honey Syrup

1   cup honey
½ cup water
¼ cup sugar
1   tablespoon lemon juice

Cream butter and sugar; add eggs, one at a time, beating well after each addition. Sift together flour, baking powder, salt, and cinnamon; add to batter. Stir in milk and orange peel. Beat well and blend in nuts. Pour into a greased and floured 9" x 13" pan. Bake at 350° F. for 30 minutes or until done. Remove from oven. Simmer honey, water, and sugar together for 5 minutes. Skim and add lemon juice; simmer 2 additional minutes. Cool. Pour syrup over cookies; refrigerate. Cut into diamonds to serve. Makes 2 dozen cookies.

North American Indians believed that honey bees brought misfortune, and called them "White man's flies," because when bees arrived, it meant that settlers had also come.

DESSERTS

Honey Raisin Pie

1½ cups raisins
1 tablespoon grated orange rind
1 cup orange juice
4 tablespoons lemon juice
¾ cup honey
2 tablespoons butter
½ teaspoon salt
4 tablespoons cornstarch
¾ cup cold water
    Pastry for double crust (9")

Rinse and drain raisins. Combine with orange rind and juice, lemon juice, honey, butter, salt, and cornstarch that has been moistened in the cold water, and stir until blended. Bring to a boil and cook and stir until mixture thickens (about 3 or 4 minutes). Pour into pastry-lined pie pan, cover with top crust. Bake in a moderately hot oven (425° F.) 30 to 35 minutes. Cool before serving.

Pumpkin Pie Filling

¾ cup strained honey
¾ cup nonfat dry milk solids
½ teaspoon salt
½ teaspoon cinnamon
½ teaspoon mace
½ teaspoon ginger
¼ teaspoon cloves
1½ cups cooked pumpkin
2 eggs, well beaten
1½ cups water
2 tablespoons melted butter
1 9" unbaked pastry shell

Mix dry ingredients well to prevent streaking. Add other ingredients. Blend thoroughly. Turn into pastry shell. Bake 15 minutes at 425° F. preheated oven. Reduce to 350° F. and bake 40 minutes longer.

In ancient Egypt, honey was offered to the gods, buried in tombs with the dead as food for the hereafter, and given to new-born babies to ward off evil spirits.

Honey Date Pudding With Lemon Sauce

¼ cup butter
1 cup honey
2 eggs
½ teaspoon vanilla
2½ cups cake flour, sifted
2½ teaspoons baking powder
½ teaspoon cinnamon
½ teaspoon ground cloves
½ teaspoon nutmeg
½ teaspoon salt
¾ cup chopped dates
½ cup pecan pieces
1 cup evaporated milk

Cream butter until light and fluffy. Add honey, eggs, and vanilla; beat 1 minute. Sift together flour, baking powder, cinnamon, cloves, nutmeg, and salt; add dates and nuts and mix until dates are flour-coated. Add milk to flour mixture; stir until well blended. Combine two mixtures; pour into buttered 5-cup mold. Cover tightly with lid that fits mold or with foil tied with strong cord. Place in pressure cooker on rack. Pour in hot water to come halfway up side of mold. Close cooker lid tightly; start cooker on high heat. Let steam escape for 30 minutes. Place pressure regulator on vent pipe; when regulator begins to rock gently, cook for an additional 45 minutes at medium heat. Remove; cool immediately with cool water. When pressure drops, remove regulator. Remove pudding; take off lid or foil. Cool slightly; remove pudding from mold. Note: If pudding is steamed on a rack in a steamer or large kettle, steam for 2 hours.

Lemon Sauce

2 tablespoons cornstarch
1¾ cups water
¾ cup honey
1 egg, well beaten
¼ teaspoon salt
¼ cup lemon juice
2 teaspoons grated lemon peel

Mix cornstarch with small amount of water. Add remaining water, honey, egg, and salt and blend well. Cook and stir until mixture thickens and comes to a boil. Remove from heat; stir in lemon juice and lemon peel.

Cranberry Pudding

2   cups large cranberries, cut in two
1½ cups flour
⅔ cup honey
⅓ cup hot water
1   teaspoon soda
½ teaspoon salt
½ teaspoon baking powder

Add dry ingredients to the cranberries mixed with the flour. Mix honey and hot water and add. Put in steamer and steam two hours. Serve with the following honey sauce.

Honey Sauce

½ cup butter
⅔ cup honey
2   tablespoons flour
2   eggs, slightly beaten
½ cup lemon juice
½ pint whipped cream

Mix and cook first four ingredients slowly in double boiler until thickened. Remove from heat. Add lemon juice. When cool and ready to serve, fold in whipped cream.

Honey Rice Pudding

⅔ cup packaged pre-cooked rice
1   cup water
¼ teaspoon salt
1¼ cups milk
1   egg yolk, slightly beaten
½ cup honey
⅛ teaspoon nutmeg
⅛ teaspoon cinnamon
1   tablespoon butter
⅓ cup raisins
    Honey Whipped Cream

Combine rice, water, and salt in saucepan. Bring to a boil, cover, and boil gently 4 minutes, or until water is absorbed. Remove from heat.

Combine milk and egg yolk; add to rice in saucepan and blend. Then add honey, spices, butter, and raisins; mix well. Bring again to a boil, stirring constantly. Cover and remove from heat. Cool to room temperature. Serve with honey sweetened whipped cream.

Honey Delight

1   package lemon or orange
        flavored gelatin
½ cup boiling water
½ cup honey
    Juice of ½ lemon
1   can evaporated milk,
        chilled and whipped
½ pound vanilla wafers, crushed

Dissolve gelatin in boiling water. Add honey and lemon juice and mix well. Fold in the evaporated milk that has been chilled and whipped. Pour this mixture into a pan that has been lined with crushed vanilla wafers. Place crushed vanilla wafers on top of mixture and put in refrigerator to set. Cut into squares.

Rhubarb and Peach Honey Cobbler

1   box (1 lb.) quick frozen
        rhubarb, thawed
1   box (10 oz.) quick frozen
        sliced peaches, thawed
1½ tablespoons quick-cooking tapioca
⅔ cup honey
1   cup sifted flour
1½ teaspoons double acting
        baking powder
2   tablespoons sugar
½ teaspoon salt
¼ teaspoon mace or nutmeg
⅓ cup butter or other shortening
¼ cup milk

Drain the rhubarb and peaches, reserving the juices. Combine juices with tapioca and bring to a boil, stirring constantly. Add honey. Remove from heat. Add rhubarb and peaches to the thickened juice. Pour into 2-quart baking dish.

Sift flour once, measure, add baking powder, sugar, salt and nutmeg, and sift again. Cut in shortening. Add milk gradually, stirring until a soft dough is formed. Turn out on lightly floured board and knead 10 seconds or enough to shape. Pat or roll dough to fit top of baking dish. Cut several slits in center and adjust dough over fruit mixture, opening slits with knife to permit escape of steam. Bake in 400° F. oven 30 minutes. Serve hot or cold, with honey sweetened whipped cream.

Honey Pecan Pie

1 cup strained honey
3 well-beaten eggs
2 tablespoons sugar
¼ cup nonfat dry milk solids
¼ cup butter
1½ cups pecan meats
½ teaspoon vanilla
1 9-inch unbaked pastry shell

Mix honey with well-beaten eggs. Cream sugar, nonfat dry milk solids, and butter and add to honey-egg mixture. Stir in pecans and vanilla. Turn into an unbaked 9″ crust and bake at 375° F. for 1 hour or until center tests done with knife. Very small muffin tins may be lined with rounds of pastry and each filled with 1 teaspoon of the above mixture. Bake 10-12 minutes at 425° F. Use for tea cakes.

French Apple Dumpling

2 cups flour
4 teaspoons baking powder
½ teaspoon salt
¼ cup lard
¾ cup milk
4 large apples
½ cup sugar
¼ teaspoon cinnamon
  melted butter

Mix ingredients as for biscuit dough. Handle as lightly as possible. Roll out the dough on a floured towel ¼″ thick. Cover the dough with the sliced apples, and sprinkle over the apples the one-half cup sugar and the cinnamon. Roll like a jelly roll and cut into 1″ slices. Place slices in a buttered baking pan. Put 1 teaspoon

melted butter over each roll. Bake at 400° F. 20 to 25 minutes. Serve with Honey Dumpling Sauce.

Honey Dumpling Sauce

1½ cups honey
2 tablespoons cornstarch
1½ cups water
⅛ teaspoon salt
1 tablespoon butter

Mix the ingredients and cook until clear. Add ½ teaspoon vanilla. Serve on the hot slices.

Honey Pumpkin Chiffon Pie

Graham Cracker Crust:

20 graham crackers (1⅔ cups)
¼ cup sifted confectioners' sugar
¼ cup soft butter

Crush the graham crackers very fine. Blend in the sugar and soft butter. Press the mixture into a heat-resistant, deep 10″ pie dish.
  Bake at 375° F. 10 minutes.

Filling:

1 tablespoon plain gelatin
¼ cup cold water
3 eggs
¾ cup honey
2 cups cooked pumpkin
½ cup whole milk
½ teaspoon salt
1 teaspoon cinnamon
½ teaspoon ginger
¼ teaspoon cloves
3 tablespoons sugar
½ pint whipping cream

Soak gelatin in cold water 5 minutes. Beat egg yolks and combine with honey, pumpkin, milk, salt and spices. Cook in top of double boiler until thick, stirring constantly. Remove from heat, add softened gelatin and stir until dissolved. Beat egg whites until frothy. Add sugar gradually and continue beating until they stand in peaks. Fold the egg whites into pumpkin mixture. Turn into graham crust and chill for several hours. Top with whipped cream.

Baked Bananas with Honey

4 firm bananas*
2 tablespoons melted butter or
   margarine
   Honey
*Use all-yellow or slightly green-tipped
bananas.

Peel bananas. Place in a well-greased baking dish. Brush bananas with honey so that entire banana is covered. Bake in a moderate oven (350° F.) for 15 to 20 minutes, or until bananas are tender . . . easily pierced with a fork. Remove from oven. With tip of spoon make a shallow groove running the length of each banana. Fill each groove with honey, about ½ teaspoon for each banana.

Honey Ice Cream Pie

1 Honey Crunch Crust
   (or a baked pie shell)
1½ quarts of ice cream
1⅓ cups flaked coconut, toasted
   Honey

Soften the ice cream slightly and fold in 1 cup of flaked coconut. Fill the prepared pie shell with scoops of the ice cream. Drizzle honey over the top, and sprinkle on the remaining flaked coconut.

Honey Crunch Crust

1 cup flaked coconut, toasted
1 cup honey-flavored puffed wheat
¼ cup honey
2 tablespoons granulated sugar
¼ teaspoon salt
1 tablespoon butter

Place coconut and cereal in a greased bowl and set aside. Combine honey, sugar, and salt in a small saucepan. Bring to a boil over medium heat, stirring to dissolve sugar. Continue boiling until small amount of syrup forms a firm ball in cold water (or to a temperature of 246° F.). Add butter. Pour syrup over coconut and cereal in bowl, stirring lightly to coat. Press mixture on bottom and sides of well-greased 9″ pie pan. Chill.

Honeycomb Pie

Pastry:
1 cup sifted all-purpose flour
⅛ teaspoon grated lemon rind
½ teaspoon salt
¼ teaspoon sugar
¼ cup shortening
2 tablespoons butter
2 to 3 tablespoons cold water

Toss together flour, lemon rind, salt and sugar in mixing bowl. Cut shortening and butter in with pastry blender or blending fork until pieces are size of rice kernels. Sprinkle water evenly over mixture and toss with fork until evenly dampened. Roll on floured board or pastry cloth into a 10″ circle. Line a 9″ pie plate with pastry, flute edge. Chill while preparing filling.

Filling:
¾ cup sifted all-purpose flour
¼ teaspoon salt
1 teaspoon baking soda
1 cup sugar
3 eggs
½ cup butter, melted
⅓ cup milk
¼ cup lemon juice
½ teaspoon grated lemon rind
1 cup honey

Sift together flour, salt and baking soda; add sugar; toss together lightly. Beat eggs until thick and lemon colored; beat in butter, milk, lemon juice, lemon rind and honey; blend well. Add dry ingredients; blend well. Pour into chilled, unbaked pie shell. Bake in a 325° F. (slow) oven for 55 to 60 minutes. Cool on cake rack. Chill before serving. Serve with whipped cream.

Honey Berry Float

1 quart milk, chilled
6 tablespoons honey
2 cups crushed fresh strawberries
½ teaspoon almond extract
1 quart vanilla ice cream

Combine milk, honey, strawberries, almond extract and one pint ice cream. Beat with rotary beater until blended. Pour into tall glasses and garnish with scoops of ice cream.

Honey Coconut Ice Cream

1 cup honey
1 envelope unflavored gelatin
2 tablespoons cold water
¼ cup brown sugar
2 eggs
3 cups light cream
1 teaspoon coconut extract or
½ teaspoon almond extract
½ cup flaked or shredded coconut

Heat honey (do not boil). Soften gelatin in water; add to honey along with sugar, eggs, cream and extract. Beat about 2 minutes. Pour into refrigerator tray. Freeze until firm, but not hard.

Turn mixture into chilled bowl. Beat until fluffy. Pour back into refrigerator tray and freeze until firm.

Toast coconut; sprinkle over each serving.

Honey Custard

¼ teaspoon salt
3 eggs, slightly beaten
¼ cup honey
2 cups milk, scalded
Nutmeg

Add salt to eggs. Beat eggs just long enough to combine whites and yolks. Add honey to milk. Add honey and milk mixture slowly to eggs. Pour into custard cups. Top with a few gratings of nutmeg. Set custard cups in pan of hot water. Bake in moderate oven (325° F.) about 40 minutes, or until custard is firm.

Tapioca Cream

⅓ cup quick cooking tapioca
⅓ cup honey
¼ teaspoon salt
2 eggs
4 cups milk, scalded
1 teaspoon vanilla extract

Combine tapioca, honey, salt, and egg yolks in top of double boiler. Add milk slowly and mix thoroughly. Cook until tapioca is transparent, stirring often. Remove from the heat and fold into the stiffly-beaten egg whites. Add the vanilla. This may be served either warm or cold with cream.

Rhubarb Tarts

2 cups rhubarb
2 egg yolks
¾ cup honey
3 tablespoons flour
¼ teaspoon salt
2 egg whites
2 tablespoons honey

Wash and cut rhubarb in ½" lengths. Pour boiling water over the rhubarb and drain in colander. Mix egg yolks (slightly beaten), honey, flour, and salt. Add to rhubarb. Pour into pastry lined muffin pans. Bake in moderate oven (350° F.) 30 minutes or until done. Top with meringue made by adding 2 tablespoons honey to 2 stiffly-beaten egg whites.

Honey-Baked Pears

Wash, halve and core pears. In a baking dish, put the juice of ½ lemon and enough water to cover bottom of pan. Place the pears, cut side down, in dish and bake covered at 375° F. for 20 minutes. At the end of 'his time, remove cover and turn pears. Drizzle pears with honey, allowing about 2 teaspoons honey per pear half. Return to oven to complete baking and to glaze pears, about 10 to 15 minutes. Serve as a meat accompaniment or as dessert with fresh cream, commercial sour cream or whipped cream, allowing 1 large half or two small halves per serving.

MEATS AND VEGETABLES

Oven-Fried Chicken with Honey Butter Sauce

1   2½ - 3 lb. broiler cut up for frying
1   cup flour
2   teaspoons salt
¼   teaspoon pepper
2   teaspoons paprika
¼   lb. or ½ cup butter
    Honey-Butter Sauce

Dip chicken pieces into mixture of flour, salt, pepper, and paprika. Melt butter in a shallow baking pan in hot oven. Remove baking pan from oven. As pieces of floured chicken are placed in pan, turn to coat with butter, then bake skin side down in a single layer. Bake at 400° F. for 30 minutes. Turn chicken. Pour Honey-Butter Sauce over chicken. Bake another 30 minutes, or until tender. Spoon Honey-Butter Sauce over chicken again.

Honey Butter Sauce

¼   cup melted butter
¼   cup honey
¼   cup lemon juice

Melt butter and beat in honey and lemon juice.

Honey-Glazed Duckling

1   5-lb. duckling
1   teaspoon salt
1   teaspoon seasoned salt
1   teaspoon poultry seasoning
½   teaspoon paprika
½   cup honey
⅓   cup orange and lemon juice
1   teaspoon dry mustard
5   thin slices lemon
5   thin slices onion

Clean duck and prick skin to allow fat to drain off when cooking. Combine salt, seasoned salt, poultry seasoning and paprika and rub inside and outside of duck. Place duck on rack in shallow pan. Place in 450° F. oven for 15 minutes; drain off fat. Reduce oven temperature to 350° F. and bake for 1 hour, draining fat as necessary. Combine honey, orange and lemon juice with mustard and brush duck with it. Secure sliced lemon and onion on duck with toothpicks; bake for 45 minutes more, brushing frequently with honey glaze.

Marinated Flank Steak

2   1½ pound flank steaks
¼   cup soy sauce
3   tablespoons honey
2   tablespoons red wine vinegar
1½ teaspoons garlic powder
1½ teaspoons ground ginger
¾   cup salad oil
1   finely chopped green onion

Combine soy sauce, honey and vinegar in a mixing bottle or jar with a tight lid. Add garlic powder and ginger. Then add salad oil and onion and mix well.

Prepare meat by stripping off excess fat. Slash lightly on the diagonal (each side) in diamond shaped cuts. Place meat in a small pan just big enough to hold it. Pour marinade over. Allow to stand at room temperature 4 hours or longer, or place in the refrigerator, covered, overnight. When ready to cook, remove steak from marinade and place on grill using medium heat. This meat cooks fast. About 6 minutes per side for medium rare.

To serve, slice thinly on the diagonal. This amount should serve 4. Or serve on buns as sandwiches.

Barbecued Spareribs

4   lbs. spareribs
½   cup chopped onion
2   garlic cloves
1½ cups catsup
2   tablespoons vinegar
½   teaspoon salt
1   teaspoon prepared mustard
½   teaspoon black pepper
2   tablespoons thick steak sauce
1   cup strained honey

Cut spareribs into serving portions. Simmer in enough water to cover, plus 2 teaspoons salt, for ½ hour. Mix the remaining ingredients and cook over low heat for 5-7 minutes. Drain spareribs and place in shallow baking pan. Pour barbecue sauce over ribs and bake in 400° F. oven for 45 minutes or until tender. Baste every 10 minutes with sauce.

In early England, France and Germany, honey was diluted with fruit juices and fermented to make "mead," an ale which made men "strong and brawny."

Honey-Fruited Pork Chops

4   double loin pork chops
1   can (8½ ounces) sliced pineapple,
      drained and reserved
½ cup honey
¼ cup pineapple syrup
1   tablespoon prepared mustard
      Maraschino cherries

Cut a pocket into each chop and insert ½ slice of pineapple. Combine honey, pineapple syrup and mustard and spoon a little over each chop. Bake at 350° F. for 1½ hours, drizzling honey sauce over the chops frequently. Remove chops from oven; top each with ½ slice of pineapple and a maraschino cherry. Return to oven for a minute or two to warm the fruit. Heat any remaining honey sauce and serve with chops.

Honey Ham Loaf

2   lbs. ground ham
1   lb. ground fresh pork
3   slices bread
½ cup milk
2   eggs
¼ cup honey
½ teaspoon cinnamon
½ teaspoon cloves

Combine ground meats in mixing bowl. Soak bread in milk and add to meat with remaining ingredients. Mix thoroughly. Mold into loaf and place in shallow roasting pan. Before baking, sprinkle ¼ cup

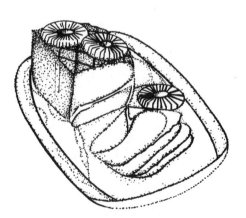

brown sugar, ¼ cup honey and 2 tablespoons vinegar over top of loaf. Bake in 350° F. oven for 2 hours.

Baked Sliced Ham with Honey Glaze

1   canned ham (5 to 6 lbs.)
      Whole cloves
¼ cup honey
¼ cup catsup
2   tablespoons prepared mustard
2   teaspoons minced onion
2   teaspoons Worcestershire sauce
¼ teaspoon lemon peel
⅛ teaspoon ginger

Have ham pre-sliced and tied securely together with string. Keep refrigerated until ready to bake. Press cloves in rows or in pattern in top of ham slices. Place on rack in shallow baking pan.

Honey Glaze

Mix together honey, catsup, mustard, onion, Worcestershire sauce, lemon peel and ginger. Spread over top and sides of ham. Bake in a 350° F. oven about 1 hour. Serve hot or cold. Garnish platter with drained canned pineapple slices and pitted cooked prunes.

Baked Ham Garnish and Glaze

1   ham
1   cup strained honey
2   large oranges
4   slices pineapple

One hour before ham is done, remove rind, score fat in large squares and cover with ½ cup honey. Let bake until glazed and lightly browned. Wash oranges, score the rind in 4 equal sections and remove carefully. With small star-shaped cutter, cut star from each section of rind. Remove as much of inner white portion as possible. Divide pulp into sections and remove fibrous covering. Place orange peel stars, orange sections and half slices of pineapple in pan with remaining honey and let cook until fruit is glazed and peel is tender. Just before ham is done, fasten a star in each square of fat with a long stemmed clove and baste with honey and fruit syrup. Garnish platter with glazed fruit and crisp parsley.

Honey Mint Lamb Sauce

½ cup water
1   tablespoon vinegar
1   cup honey
¼ cup chopped mint

Heat water and vinegar. Add honey, stir well, then add chopped mint. Cook slowly for five minutes. This sauce can be used to baste lamb chops or lamb roast during cooking or can be served with meat at the table.

Honey-Baked Squash

1   acorn squash
4 or 6 small pork links
4   teaspoons honey

Wash squash, cut in halves and remove seeds. Place two teaspoons honey in each half. Also place two or three cooked and drained pork links in each half.

Bake in oven at 350° F. for 30 to 40 minutes or until squash is done.

Citrus Honey Carrots

1   bunch carrots
    Salt
¼ cup melted butter or margarine
¼ cup honey
1½ teaspoons grated orange peel
1½ teaspoons grated lemon peel

Wash and scrape carrots; cook in 1" of boiling salted water until crispy-tender; about 15 to 20 minutes. Drain. Blend melted butter, honey and citrus peels. Pour over cooked carrots and place over low heat until carrots are thoroughly glazed.

Honey-Baked Beans

2   cups dried beans
½ pound scored salt pork
1   tablespoon onion, chopped
1   teaspoon ginger
½ cup honey
1   teaspoon salt
1   teaspoon dry mustard

Soak washed beans in 4 cups warm water 3 hours. Cook on low heat in tightly-covered saucepan 1¼ hours. Do not allow to boil. Drain the beans, saving the water. Place salt pork in the bottom of bean pot and add beans. Cover with mixture made of the bean water, onion, ginger, honey, salt and mustard. Add boiling water, if needed. Place small pieces of salt pork on top, cover pot and bake in slow oven about 6 hours. Uncover bean pot during last hour of baking. If the beans become too dry, add a little boiling water.

Candied Sweet Potatoes

Boil 6 medium-sized sweet potatoes without paring them. When tender drain and remove skins. Cut in half lengthwise and arrange in buttered baking dish. Season with salt. Heat ¼ cup butter, ½ cup honey, ½ cup orange juice, add to potatoes. Bake in oven 400° F. until potatoes are brown.

Favorite Candied Yams

1½ cups honey
2   tablespoons cornstarch
⅛ teaspoon salt
1½ cups water
1   tablespoon butter
6   large sliced and cooked yams

Mix and cook all ingredients except yams until mixture is clear. Pour over cooked sweet potatoes and bake at 400° F. until brown. Also very good over baked apples.

Fluffy Sweet Potato Casserole

6   medium-sized sweet potatoes
¼ cup butter
¼ cup brown sugar
¼ cup honey
1   tablespoon grated orange rind
½ teaspoon salt
½ cup chopped pecans
    Marshmallows
    Orange sections

Cook sweet potatoes in boiling water until tender; drain and mash. Combine mashed sweet potatoes with butter, brown sugar, honey, grated orange rind and salt; fold in pecans and mix well. Pile mixture in baking casserole which has been greased with shortening or butter. Garnish with marshmallows and orange sections. Bake in moderate oven 350° F. 30 to 35 minutes or until thoroughly heated.

SALADS AND DRESSINGS

Banana Fruit Dressing

1   ripe banana, mashed
3   tablespoons honey
¼ cup orange juice
¼ teaspoon salt
½ cup buttermilk

Combine banana, honey, orange juice, and salt; gradually stir in buttermilk; whip with a rotary beater until smooth. Chill. Serve with fresh fruit salad.

Honey Cranberry Relish

2   cups fresh cranberries
1   orange
1   cup honey

Sort and wash cranberries. Wash and quarter orange. Put orange and cranberries through food chopper. Add honey and mix well. Let stand overnight. Chill before serving.

Walnut Jewel Salad

1   3 oz. package pineapple-flavored
    gelatin
1   cup hot water
½ teaspoon salt
1   cup cold liquid (drained pineapple
    juice plus water)
1   cup chopped raw cranberries
½ cup canned crushed pineapple,
    drained
½ cup diced celery
½ cup chopped California walnuts

Dissolve gelatin in hot water. Add salt and cold water - drained - pineapple - juice mixture. Chill until slightly thickened. Fold in remaining ingredients. Turn into a one-quart mold or into eight individual molds. Chill until firm. Unmold onto bed of crisp lettuce, decorate with additional walnut halves or pieces, and serve with Honey-Creme Salad Dressing.

Honey-Creme Salad Dressing

1   3 oz. package cream cheese
¼ teaspoon salt
2   tablespoons honey
¼ cup dairy sour cream

In a small bowl, whip or mash cream cheese with salt, honey and sour cream. For smoother dressing, whip with electric beater.

Honey Of A Dressing

Add ¼ cup honey to ¾ cup sour cream. Mix gently and thoroughly.

Banana Nut Ambrosia

2   bananas, cut crosswise
4   maraschino cherries, cut in half
¼ cup mayonnaise
2   tablespoons honey
1   tablespoon pineapple juice
¼ cup chopped nuts
¼ cup shredded coconut

Arrange sliced bananas and cherries on greens. Mix mayonnaise, honey and juice and spoon over fruit. Sprinkle nuts and coconut on top.

Honey Cheese Dressing

½ cup cottage cheese
2   tablespoons honey
1   teaspoon grated lemon rind
1¼ tablespoons lemon juice
½ teaspoon salt
½ cup salad oil

Force cottage cheese through sieve, add honey, lemon rind, juice and salt and beat briskly with egg beater. Add oil, a teaspoon at a time, until half the oil is used, blending well between each addition. Add remaining oil 2 tablespoons at a time. A delicious dressing for fruit salads or avocados.

Fruit French Dressing

⅓ cup honey
1   teaspoon salt
1   teaspoon paprika
1   cup unsweetened pineapple juice
2   well-beaten eggs
2   three-ounce packages cream cheese
¼ cup orange juice
2½ tablespoons lemon juice

Mix dry ingredients; add honey and fruit juices, blend. Cook in double boiler 20 minutes, stirring constantly. Slowly stir into eggs. Cook 5 minutes, stirring constantly. Cool slightly. Soften cream cheese; beat in cooked mixture. Chill.

Honey Dressing

⅔ cup sugar
1 teaspoon dry mustard
1 teaspoon paprika
1 teaspoon celery seed
¼ teaspoon salt
⅓ cup strained honey
5 tablespoons vinegar
1 tablespoon lemon juice, fresh,
   frozen or canned
1 teaspoon grated onion
1 cup salad oil

Mix dry ingredients; add honey, vinegar, lemon juice and onion. Pour oil into mixture very slowly, beating constantly with rotary or electric beater or in blender.

Pink Shrimp-Orange Salad

3 medium oranges, peeled, cut into
   bite-size pieces (1½ cups)
½ cup sliced celery
½ cup sliced ripe olives
½ pound cleaned, cooked shrimp
2 tablespoons chopped onion
¼ teaspoon salt
Citrus Honey Dressing

Combine orange pieces, celery, olives, shrimp, chopped onion, and salt; blend with a little Citrus Honey Dressing to moisten. Chill. Serve in lettuce cup on individual salad plates with Citrus Honey Dressing.

Citrus Honey Dressing.

¼ cup honey
½ cup mayonnaise
1 tablespoon grated orange peel
3 tablespoons fresh orange juice
1 tablespoon fresh lemon juice
½ teaspoon paprika

Combine all ingredients, blending well.

Honey Cabbage Salad

1 medium head cabbage, shredded
1 medium cantaloupe
5 minted pear halves
Strawberries and minted leaves

Shred cabbage and crisp in ice water for 10 minutes. Drain and dry thoroughly.

Use minted pears or add a drop of mint extract and green coloring to pear syrup. Let the pear halves absorb the color and flavor. Remove rind and seeds of the cantaloupe. Save one half for cutting into slices for garnish. Cut the remainder into ½" cubes. Toss cabbage and cantaloupe cubes with Honey-Soy Dressing. Garnish with cantaloupe slices, pear halves trimmed with strawberries and mint.

Honey-Soy Dressing

½ cup fresh lemon juice
⅓ cup honey
½ teaspoon grated lemon rind
1 drop mint extract
½ cup oil
2 tablespoons toasted sesame seeds
1 teaspoon chutney
½ teaspoon soy sauce
Dash of salt

Shake ingredients together in a covered jar. Chill.

Pear Sunshine Tray

5 canned Bartlett pear halves
5 canned Freestone peach halves
5 dates
5 walnut halves
1 grapefruit, sectioned
1 red apple, sliced grapes
Salad greens

Drain juice from the can of pears. Arrange fruits on a bed of crisp salad greens with stuffed dates atop the peach halves. Serve with Honey French Dressing.

Honey French Dressing

¼ cup honey
¼ cup lemon juice
¼ cup salad oil
½ cup pear juice
Few grains salt
½ teaspoon celery seed
¼ teaspoon dry mustard

Combine ingredients in jar and shake until well blended.

A pharaoh who lived more than 2000 years before the Exodus is believed to have introduced the honey bee into Egypt.

Poppy Seed Salad Dressing

⅓ cup strained honey
½ teaspoon salt
⅓ cup vinegar
3 tablespoons mustard
1¼ cups salad oil
2½ tablespoons poppy seeds

Mix together in the order given. Blend in an electric blender or mixer until oil disappears.

Honey-Glazed Orange Slices

¼ cup honey
¼ teaspoon nutmeg (optional)
2 tablespoons butter or margarine
8 orange slices ¼" thick
Whole cloves

Blend honey, butter and nutmeg in a skillet until butter is melted. Stud orange rind with cloves. Simmer orange slices in honey. Glaze 15 minutes. Turn frequently to glaze evenly. Serve with roast duckling.

Honey-Lime Dressing

1 6 oz. can frozen limeade concentrate
¾ cup salad oil
½ cup honey
¼ teaspoon salt
2 teaspoons celery seed

Put limeade, salad oil, honey, and salt in a blender container; blend a few seconds. Stir in celery seed. (Mixture may be beaten or shaken to mix.) Serve over fresh or canned fruit salad.

Creamy Honey Dressing

3 oz. package of cream cheese
⅓ cup cider vinegar
¼ cup honey
½ teaspoon cinnamon
1 teaspoon paprika
1 teaspoon salt
¼ cup salad oil

Blend cream cheese and vinegar. Add honey and seasonings. Mix well and whip in salad oil.

Lemon-Lime Dressing

2 eggs, beaten
¼ cup lemon juice
¼ cup lime juice
⅔ cup honey
½ teaspoon salt
1 tablespoon snipped chives or parsley
1 cup sour cream

Mix eggs, juices and honey in little saucepan. Stir over low heat until thickened. Let cool a bit. Mix remaining ingredients, then fold into egg mixture. Chill.

Avocado and Fruit Salad

1 avocado, chilled and peeled
2 grapefruit, chilled and peeled, sectioned
2-3 oranges, chilled, peeled, sectioned

Cut avocado in half crosswise, remove seed, slice into thin circles; cut each circle in half. On individual lettuce-lined salad plates alternately arrange grapefruit and avocado sections, rounded edges up. Place orange sections around other fruits. Garnish with watercress and ripe olives. Serve with Honey French Dressing.

Honey French Dressing

⅓ cup salad oil
2 tablespoons vinegar
¼ teaspoon salt
⅛ teaspoon paprika
2 tablespoons strained honey

Combine ingredients. Shake well.

In Roman mythology, Amor, the god of love, dipped his arrows in honey.

HONEY COOKING TIPS

All the recipes in this book have been prepared and taste-tested using honey. However, when substituting honey for sugar in your other recipes, follow these general guidelines:

- Substitute equal amounts of honey for sugar up to one cup.

- Reduce total amount of other liquids by ¼ cup per cup of honey.

- Lower baking temperature 25° to prevent overbrowning.

Two tablespoons of honey added to your favorite cake mix will make the cake wonderfully tender and less crumbly. (For best results, add the honey in a fine stream to the batter as you beat.)

Foods sweetened with honey will have a better flavor if kept until the day after baking before serving.

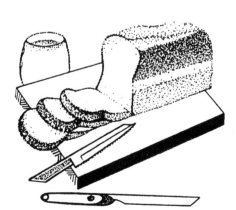

Honey crystallizes — that's its nature! Taste or purity is NOT affected . . . in fact, it makes a delicious crunchy spread in this form. To bring crystallized honey back to its natural liquid state, place container of honey in a pan of warm water (not hot!) until crystals disappear.

When using honey in cooking, moisten the measuring spoon or cup first with water or oil, then measure the honey. This will eliminate sticking.

Store honey at room temperature, not in the refrigerator. Keep container closed and in a dry place.

If you're baking goodies for children away at school, young men overseas, or friends out of town, honey will help your baked goods stay oven-fresh because of its marvelous "keeping" qualities.

For a delicious treat, pour honey over cereal, fruit or ice cream, or mix it with milk for a nutritious, tasty drink.

To neutralize honey's natural acidity, add 1/12 teaspoon of baking soda to the ingredients per cup of honey. However, when sour milk is used with honey in a recipe, you may omit the extra soda.

In ancient times, honey was considered so valuable that it was often used in place of gold to pay taxes.

HONEY HEALTH HINTS

Use honey in infant formulas to provide a wholesome sugar, supplementary minerals, an antiseptic and a mild laxative. It also has a definite beneficial influence upon calcium retention.

♦ ♦ ♦

Honey used as a sweetener does not result in heavy production of body fat as does refined sugar. It is palatable and digestible as well as nutritious.

♦ ♦ ♦

Many nutrition experts consider honey excellent nourishment, or a "power supply" for the heart muscle.

♦ ♦ ♦

Besides being an unexcelled energy food, honey is one of nature's most powerful germ killers. Germs simply cannot survive in honey. In fact, primitive man not only used honey as food, but also as medicine to heal his wounds.

♦ ♦ ♦

Mixed with lemon juice, honey is an excellent remedy for simple coughs.

♦ ♦ ♦

Honey is a natural laxative, and one of the fastest-working stimulants known.

♦ ♦ ♦

Honey is a natural, unrefined food, unique in that it is the ONLY unmanufactured sweet available in commercial quantities.

♦ ♦ ♦

Sugars form 75 to 80 percent of honey. When ordinary sugars like cane or beet are consumed, they must be broken down by digestive juices before they can be absorbed into the blood stream and assimilated by the tissues. With honey, little digestion is necessary, so absorption and the resulting energy boost occur quickly. (This is one reason honey is so nutritious for athletes or anyone who needs instant energy.)

♦ ♦ ♦

Because honey is 99 percent naturally predigested as it comes, it puts little or no strain on the digestive system.

A scotch whiskey base, honey, and special herbs and spices result in the crown jewel of all liqueurs—Drambuie.

Additional Notes and Recipes

Additional Notes and Recipes

Additional Notes and Recipes

Additional Notes and Recipes

The Following Amounts Will Serve Approximately 40 Persons

1 pound coffee

1 quart cream

1 pound honey—will sweeten
   coffee for 40

10 quarts milk

1 pound butter or margarine

1 quart honey French dressing

1 peck potatoes

2 10-pound honey-baked hams

80 honey rolls

2 quarts sandwich filling

6 quarts salad

6 pounds cabbage (for salad)

1 quart honey mayonnaise

5 pounds dried beans

2 quarts olives

2 gallons honey ice cream

4 9-inch honey layer cakes
   (serves 40 generously)

2 dozen medium-sized lemons ⎫ makes honey
2 pounds honey   ⎬ lemonade for 40
8 quarts water   ⎭

3 pints honey jam

1 peck sweet potatoes

Useful Equivalents

		approximately
2	cups fat	1 pound
2¼	cups brown sugar, firmly packed	1 pound
3½	cups confectioners' sugar	1 pound
4	cups flour (sifted)	1 pound
4½	cups cake flour (sifted)	1 pound
3½	cups graham flour	1 pound
½	cup evaporated milk and ½ cup water	1 cup milk
8	to 10 egg whites	1 cup egg whites
1	square unsweetened chocolate	1 ounce
3½	tablespoons cocoa and ½ tablespoon butter	1 square chocolate
1	tablespoon cornstarch	2 tablespoons flour (thickening)
4	to 5 lemons	1 cup juice
1	pound peanut butter	1⅔ cups
14	to 16 slices bacon	1 pound
2½	cups raisins	1 pound
1	cup raw rice	3 cups cooked
1	package macaroni (8 oz.)	4 cups cooked
2½	cups dates	1 pound
3	cups figs (chopped)	1 pound
3½	cups walnuts (chopped)	1 pound

Old Favorite Ways to Use Honey au naturel

SUNDAY—   Hot Biscuits and honey for breakfast
                  Waffles with warm honey for supper
EVERY DAY—Cereal with honey
                  Fruit with honey
                  Bread and butter with honey
                  Milk and honey for a nutritious and tasty
                    beverage

INDEX
Old Favorite Honey Recipes
and the
Honey Recipes Book